Becoming A Man Of Integrity:

A Study on the Life of Joseph

Paul E. Robinson

Becoming a Man of Integrity:
A Study on the Life of Joseph
Copyright © 2016 by Paul E. Robinson

ISBN-13: 978-1533193513
ISBN-10: 1533193517

Cover Design © 2016 by Richard M. Robinson
Edited by Donna Robinson
Scripture quotations from the King James Version

All rights reserved. No part of this publication
may be reproduced or transmitted for commercial
purposes, except for brief quotations in printed
reviews, without written permission from the publisher.

Published by
Robin 5 Publishing
P.O. Box 963
Eastlake, CO 80614

Printed in the United States of America

*"And the LORD was with Joseph,
and he was a prosperous man..."*
Genesis 39:2

Table of Contents

Introduction 7

1. Joseph's Premonitions: His Dreams 13

2. Joseph's Persecution: His Rejection 27

3. Joseph's Prosperity: His Testimony 43

4. Joseph's Plight: His Character 57

5. Joseph's Predictions: His Compassion 77

6. Joseph's Patience: His Waiting 87

7. Joseph's Puzzle: His Faith 101

8. Joseph's Power: His Triumph 119

9. Joseph's Purpose: His Interrogations 129

10. Joseph's Promise: His Forgiveness 153

Conclusion 171

Joseph, a Perfect Type of Christ 181

Introduction

The last of the four patriarchs of Genesis, Joseph was different from the rest, most notably because he was not in the line of Christ. Yet the story of Joseph is one of the most famous in all the Bible. The events of the story are incredible, but the most amazing part is Joseph himself.

Abraham, Isaac, Jacob, and Joseph were the four patriarchs of Genesis, the focal points of the book. **Abraham was the devotee**, a true worshipper of God who had great faith. He is often called the Father of Faith. **Isaac was the digger**. Only one chapter is completely devoted to him, and we see him digging wells and fighting for territory. **Jacob was the deceiver**. He tricked his brother and deceived his own father into getting the family blessing. It took a long time, but he eventually learned to trust God, and the Lord changed his name to Israel, meaning "prince with God."

But Joseph was different from his ancestors. **Joseph was the dreamer**. He had two notable dreams as a young man, and he clung to those dreams, believing that God would eventually fulfill them. Joseph was the most insignificant of the family, yet he grew to become one of the most important men in the world at that time. Truly, God delights in using *"the weak things of the world to confound the things which are mighty"* (I Cor. 1:27b).

Joseph had something that the other patriarchs did not have: integrity. Abraham lied about his wife twice. Isaac was a fleshly man in his old age, depending entirely on his senses and not on the Lord. Jacob gave in to deceit, a sin which came back to bite him when his Uncle Laban tricked him, and his own sons fooled him into thinking Joseph was dead. We never find Joseph lying, trusting his flesh, or being deceitful. In fact, we never even see him complain! Joseph suffered rejection, false accusations, and abandonment, yet he maintained his integrity throughout these trials.

No doubt God chose Joseph because He saw he was a man of integrity. Joseph's brothers had no such morals; they were selfish, greedy, and inconsiderate. God needed a man who had convictions, high morals, and real compassion. Joseph was that man. Yet God tested Joseph to bring those qualities out completely. If you believe that you're a man of integrity, God will test you to discover what you're made of. He wants all the dross to melt away so He can use you effectively.

While not in the Messianic line, Joseph was given more time and attention in the Bible than any of the other patriarchs. In fact, the last quarter of the book of Genesis is completely devoted to Joseph. Why would the Holy Spirit focus on this man? I believe there are two main reasons.

First, remember who wrote this book (humanly speaking): Moses. Moses must have heard the story of Joseph from his mother when he was living in Egypt. His mother was able to nurture him and take care of him under Pharaoh's daughter for many years. She must have thought the story of Joseph would be a profitable one for Moses, a man who would grow up in Pharaoh's household. The story of Joseph was a precious one to the Israelites; after all, it explained how they came to live in Egypt. With every fact and detail rushing back into Moses' mind, he penned the story of Joseph in the Word of God.

Second, and more importantly, Joseph was the single greatest type of Jesus Christ in the Bible. Almost every aspect of his life showed a type of Christ's life. While Joseph was not in the line of Christ, God still chose to use him in this amazing way as a type of our blessed Savior. If you study the life of Joseph, you will find over fifty parallels between his life and the life of Jesus! Joseph gives us the fullest picture of Christ in the Old Testament.

Once again, it was his integrity which set Joseph apart. To find a man of such high integrity in the Bible is rare indeed. Even David, the man after God's own heart, did not have such integrity. God is looking for such men today. God does not want men with money, or men with talent, or men with influence. He wants men with integrity, who prize Biblical convictions, honesty, faith, and compassion.

We have much to learn from the life of Joseph. It is full of powerful lessons for the men and women of today. Joseph's life was tested, true, and timeless. It is exactly the kind of life we should all desire to live.

One
Joseph's Premonitions
His Dreams

"And Joseph dreamed a dream, and he told it his brethren: and they hated him yet the more."
Genesis 37:5

The land of Canaan. Although Jacob was a stranger in this land, it was where God wanted him to live. It was this land which Abraham sought by faith, which Isaac fought for territory over, and where Jacob escaped after dealing with his wily Uncle Laban. This land was where he would raise his sons.

It was in the land of Canaan that little Joseph grew up. Although he had ten older brothers, he was the firstborn of Rachel, Jacob's favorite wife. As a result, Joseph was Jacob's favorite son. He even made Joseph a special coat of many colors to prove it. This did not go over too well with his brothers. *"And when his brethren saw that their father loved him more than all his brethren, they hated him, and could not speak peaceably to him"* (Gen. 37:4). They gave him the cold shoulder. He had done nothing wrong; he was simply the favorite son.

Joseph grew up in a dysfunctional home. His mother died when he was very young. He had three step-mothers, who most likely did not love him. His brothers were wild and worldly. Genesis 37:2 tells us that Joseph brought an evil report to his father concerning them.

Life was not easy for Joseph. Yet he had one good thing in his life: his father, who loved him unconditionally. Joseph readily listened to and obeyed his father in Genesis 37. Joseph was not a brat, he was an obedient son, probably the only son in the family who had good character. So when Joseph received that colorful coat, he was proud to wear it. It was a symbol of his strong relationship with his loving father. It was the best thing he had in life.

In the Bible, Joseph's story begins when he was only seventeen years old (vs. 2). What an important age for a young person! This is the age of decision, the age of preparation before striking out on the path of independence and responsibility. We find Joseph doing all the right things. He gave an honest report to his father concerning his brothers. This caused his brothers to despise him, seeing him only as "the tattle-tale." He was a hard worker, no doubt getting stuck with the brunt of the work while his brothers ran off to do something else.

At such a young age, Joseph was already a man of integrity and honesty. God looked down from heaven. He looked among the sons of Jacob and found one who had character. Scripture clearly states, *"For the eyes of the LORD run to and fro throughout the whole earth, to shew himself strong in the behalf of them whose heart is perfect toward him…"* (II Chron. 16:9). God had a plan for Jacob's family, and He needed Joseph for that plan.

Consider your life. Whether young or old, you have no idea what God has in store for you. The Lord is looking for men and women with integrity. Do you do your job, working hard? Are you honest and fair? These are qualities God is looking for! They are in short supply today. Will God find such a person in you?

One night, Joseph laid his head on his pillow to go to sleep. Little did he know something would happen that would change the rest of his life.

Joseph's First Dream

During that night, Joseph had a dream. It was a very peculiar dream. In the morning, he was eager to share this dream with his family. His disgruntled brothers reluctantly listened.

"Wait 'til you guys hear this! In my dream, we were binding up sheaves in the field like we usually do, and suddenly my sheaf stood up straight! And then, all your sheaves came over and bowed down to my sheaf!"

Joseph's brothers did not appreciate this dream. *"And his brethren said to him, Shalt thou indeed reign over us? or shalt thou indeed have dominion over us?"* (vs. 8a). What were they talking about? It was just a dream. But those snarky brothers knew that dreams meant something. Back then, God often spoke to people through dreams. Perhaps not every dream, but some dreams could be vitally important in a mysterious way.

Joseph's dream had an obvious meaning: his brothers would one day bow down to him and make obeisance to him. Looking at the brat, they could never imagine doing such a thing. Why would they ever bow down to him? So they pushed the dream away, calling it nonsense. Perhaps even Joseph turned away from his thoughts, thinking it was too good to be true. But God would confirm this truth to Joseph through the same means.

Joseph's Second Dream

The Bible does not tell us when he dreamed the second dream; perhaps it was the next night, or perhaps a week later. It was no doubt soon after the first. God used this second dream to confirm that the message was true. Joseph woke up, excited to share the news. This time, he told it to his brothers *and* his father Jacob.

Joseph ran to them, caught his breath, and said, "Listen, everyone! I had another dream last night! This time, the sun and the moon and eleven stars bowed down to me!" This dream was far more ridiculous than the first. The implications were huge. The first dream had to do with his family bowing down to him, but this one gave the sense that all the universe would bow down to him. In other words, the whole world would one day worship Joseph!

Jacob lovingly rebuked his favorite son. *"... and his father rebuked him, and said unto him, What is this dream that thou hast dreamed? Shall I and thy mother and thy brethren indeed come to bow down ourselves to thee to the earth?"* (vs. 10). Jacob found this hard to believe. How would Joseph ever get into a position where the whole world would bow down to him? Jacob left out a big piece of the puzzle: God. The Lord had all the pieces to Joseph's life. He simply needed to fit them in the right places to make a beautiful picture. Remember, Christian, although your life is a puzzle, God is the One putting it together.

Joseph's second dream had two different responses. The brothers responded with envy. "What's so special about Joseph?" They probably taunted him and ridiculed him by calling him names, such as "the little dreamer." They had another reason to envy him now. Not only was

Joseph "Daddy's boy," but now he had special dreams which he claimed would come true some day. They despised him and hated him even more.

The other response came from Joseph's father, who observed the saying. Jacob had experienced his own important dream when he was in Bethel. In Genesis 28, Jacob laid down to sleep and dreamed of angels going up and down a ladder to heaven. In this dream, God spoke directly to Jacob. Now his son was having dreams, and Jacob couldn't help but wonder if the Lord was speaking to his boy.

As for Joseph, he clung to his dreams. Now he had something besides his father's love; he had something from God, which Joseph believed would one day become reality. Despite the ridicule, he held on. He had something physical (his colorful coat) and now something spiritual.

Do You Have Dreams?

God does not speak to us through dreams and visions today because we have the entire canon of Scripture. Yet we can certainly dream! And it may be that God has put a dream in your heart. Every person needs to dream, and they need to hold onto that dream despite the opposition and ridicule.

Walt Disney had a dream. It was a dream of a place, a "magical park," where children and parents could have fun together. Originally Disney planned on using eight acres of land next to the Burbank studios where his employees would often go to relax. However, during World War II, he realized that eight acres would not be enough.

In 1953, Disney had the Stanford Research Institute conduct a survey for a 100-acre site outside of Los Angeles. His dream expanded in his mind: he could see flying elephants, giant teacups, a fairy tale castle, moon rockets, all contained in a magical kingdom he would call "Disneyland."

Disney's dream quickly met opposition. Finding the right spot was difficult, but they eventually settled on a 160-acre stretch of land near the junction of the Santa Ana Freeway and Harbor Boulevard. Disneyland would be expensive. Walt once said, "I could never convince the financiers that Disneyland was feasible, because dreams offer too little collateral."

Tons of trees and fifteen houses were moved in order to prepare for construction. Despite problems and time constraints, work progressed. If Disney did not like something, he would take it upon himself to do the job right, as in the case of the Tom Sawyers Island design. Bit by bit, Disneyland came together, making Disney's dream a reality.

Finally in the summer of 1955, Disneyland opened. The first day saw 28,000 people come through the gates. Disney had this to say to those who entered the park, "To all that come to this happy place: welcome. Disneyland is your land. Here age relives fond memories of the past, and here youth may savor the challenge and promise of the future. Disneyland is dedicated to the ideals, the dreams, and the hard facts that have created America. . . with hope that it will be a source of joy and inspiration to all the world."

Walt Disney saw his dream become a reality. He did not give up because of opposition, both financial and foundational. He saw his dream through to the end. He clung to that dream, using it to inspire him to keep going.

But Disney had another dream. In 1965, he announced that he wanted to build a bigger and better park than Disneyland. This park would be located in Orlando, Florida. Much planning and work went into the new park, but Disney would not live to see it open. He died in 1966 of acute circulatory collapse, caused by lung cancer. Despite the fact that he was gone, his dream lived on and became a reality. Disney World opened in 1971. Even in his absence, Disney's dream came true.

Let me put this on a more personal level. When I was a little boy, I had a dream of being a preacher. I wanted to be just like my preacher dad. I would see him get in the pulpit and preach, and I wanted to do the same when I grew up. I believe God put this dream in my heart even before I was saved. After my salvation at the age of ten, I continued to pursue this dream. I preached in competitions in high school, my dad helping me and teaching me how to preach.

Finally, I graduated from high school and went off to Bible college to get my pastoral degree. I loved college! I grew to love preaching even more, and God developed me into a preacher. After college, God burdened my heart to move back home and become the youth pastor for my church, and that is what I am currently doing. I'm a preacher today, but I'm still holding onto that dream of one day pastoring a church of my own. This is my dream, and I will cling to it, believing that God will one day fulfill it, making it a reality in my life.

The question is, dear Christian, do you dream? What dream are you holding onto? It's sad to think that so many people live their lives without any dreams. They wake up, go to work, come home, eat, and go to sleep. Life is boring if you have nothing to live for. I see people who have no ambition in life. What they need is a dream, something they can reach for.

Dream Big

Has *God* given you this dream? Joseph's dreams were directly from God, and he held onto those dreams until they came true.

It's common to ask kids what they want to be when they grow up. Usually they say they want to be a policeman or a fireman, something exciting. You never hear a kid say he wants to be a retail manager or a McDonald's employee. He wants to have an exciting career that makes a difference in people's lives. While some kids never see these dreams come true, others passionately pursue theirs, becoming what they had always dreamed about.

It's not enough to just have dreams, you must pursue them. Eleanor Roosevelt stated, "The future belongs to those who believe in the beauty of their dreams." What can you do to make that dream come true? As you do so, pray and ask God to lead you. If God has given you that dream, it will one day come true.

Joseph was severely tested before his dreams were fulfilled. It may be that God will do the same for your dreams. Do you really want them? Will you do anything in order for those dreams to become a reality?

This is where many people give up. "I wanted to be a doctor, but it's too much work." They're not willing to make the investment of time and work in order to see that dream materialize. A dream that is easily achieved is easily forgotten. Helen Keller made this amazing statement: "The most pathetic person in the world is someone who has sight but no vision."

So let me ask you again: Has God given you a dream? If you believe it is from the Lord, then pursue it. Work for it. Don't be afraid that it won't come true. Consider the wonderful promise of I Thessalonians 5:24: *"Faithful is he that calleth you, who also will do it."* God has called you, and has given you a dream. He will see it to the end.

The first lesson we learn from Joseph is to dream. More than anything, Joseph was a dreamer. His dreams were his foundation for everything else. In other words, he believed that God would fulfill them.

Dear reader, are you a dreamer? Do you need ambition in your life? Ask God to give you a dream. Or maybe it's time to finally pursue that dream you've been putting off. Don't let anything stop you.

Two
Joseph's Persecution
His Rejection

"And it came to pass, when Joseph was come unto his brethren, that they stript Joseph out of his coat of many colours that was on him; And they took him, and cast him into a pit..."

Genesis 37:23-24

Rejection is a very real problem in the world today. Many people experience rejection from their family or friends. Perhaps you have experienced the pain of being rejected. A person is often rejected for one of two reasons: (1) he is handicapped in some way (as in blind, crippled) or (2) he is envied because of something he has that others do not. The latter was true for Joseph. Joseph was envied by his brothers because he was his father's favorite son, and this led to rejection and persecution.

Joseph had done nothing wrong to be treated the way he was. It was not his fault that his father loved him most. His brothers' hatred for him only grew when he told them his dreams. Perhaps you have been rejected by your family for your dreams or ambitions. They think you're a fool for believing them and pursuing them. The truth is, they are jealous that they don't have such aspirations, but they dare not tell you.

Let's not sugar-coat the reality of rejection. It is the most deadly weapon that can be used in a family. No child wants to be rejected by his parents or siblings. Child abuse, whether verbal or physical, is detrimental to that child because he wants to be accepted by his parents. An abusive father or an uncaring mother are the worst dream-destroyers in the world.

Rejection by peers can also be devastating. Suicide is a sad reality in our world today, and many teens have committed suicide after being harshly rejected by their schoolmates. Had those schoolmates realized how deadly their persecution was, they would have never pursued it.

No one wants to be rejected. Lance Armstrong

admitted a simple truth when he stated, "A boo is a lot louder than a cheer." Actor Harrison Ford once observed, "Some actors couldn't figure out how to withstand the constant rejection. They couldn't see the light at the end of the tunnel." The truth is, we should be prepared for rejection. Actor Sylvester Stallone admitted, "I take rejection as someone blowing a bugle in my ear to wake me up and get going, rather than retreat."

Joseph was rejected by his ten brothers. His mother was gone, but he had the love of his father, and now he had two precious dreams from God. Joseph held onto that love and those dreams while trying to ignore the hatred of his own siblings. But little did he realize that their hatred for him would soon climax with a despicable act.

The Hatred of Rejection

Rejection usually begins with hatred over the other person's abilities, gifts, talents, or simply the circumstances he has. In Joseph's case, his brothers hated him because he was their father's favorite. But their hatred grew. *"And they hated him yet the more for his dreams, and for his words"* (Gen. 37:8b).

One day Joseph's ten brothers went to feed the sheep in Shechem. Jacob called for Joseph, and told him to check up on his brothers. Joseph obeyed his father but when he arrived at Shechem, he could not find them. As Joseph wandered around in the field, a man approached him and asked what he was looking for. Joseph replied that he's looking for his brothers, and the man stated that they left for Dothan.

Right there we see Joseph's integrity on display. He had gone to where he thought his brothers would be, to the place his father told him to go. It would have been easy to say, "Well, they're not here, so I'll go home and tell Father." Instead, Joseph kept going. He would not return to his father without a report about his brothers. He was a young man of obedience. Contrast this with his brothers, who were not even at the place they were supposed to be.

Joseph finally arrived in Dothan and saw his brothers in the distance. He was probably relieved to see they hadn't gone off to another place. But the brothers could also see Joseph in the distance, and as he approached, their hatred for him transformed into another monstrosity.

The Bitterness of Rejection

Hatred, if left unchecked, will always lead to bitterness, which will in turn lead to something horrible. That's exactly what happened here. *"And when they saw him afar off, even before he came near unto them, they conspired against him to slay him"* (vs. 18). They wanted to kill Joseph. It didn't matter that he was their brother. Their hatred for him had brought out their worst desires, the ones that had been buried deep in their hearts. *"And they said one to another, Behold, this dreamer cometh"* (vs. 19). They said it mockingly, envious and bitter against the favorite son.

Notice the bitterness of their next statement: *"Come now therefore, and let us slay him, and cast him into some pit, and we will say, Some evil beast hath devoured him: and we shall see what will become of his dreams"* (vs. 20). What bitterness they displayed!

The Bible warns against bitterness. Hebrews 12:15 says, *"Looking diligently lest any man fail of the grace of God; lest any root of bitterness springing up trouble you, and thereby many be defiled."* Bitterness is planted deep in the heart, and often hatred is the planter. If you don't uproot it, bitterness will grow until it comes out in your life, and many people will be "defiled," that is, they will be hurt. Your bitterness will hurt the person you're bitter against, but it will also hurt others. In Joseph's case, the bitterness of the brothers deeply hurt Jacob, who mourned many days for his son and refused to be comforted (vs. 34-35).

Joseph would have quickly been killed if not for Reuben, the oldest of his brothers. Reuben stepped in, suggesting they cast him into a pit so that later he could get him out and bring him back to his father. Reuben was a compromiser. He wanted to appease his brothers, but he also wanted to keep Joseph alive and bring him home safely. Here Reuben showed weak leadership. Any leader who chooses to compromise, especially over someone's life, is weak.

Although the Bible does not say it, the brothers agreed with Reuben. They would not kill Joseph, but simply throw him into a pit and watch him suffer. And they would enjoy every second of it.

The Climax of Rejection

When you store bitterness and hatred in your heart, it will only grow and eventually burst into some type of action. After envying the dreamer, the brothers became hateful, then bitter, and all of this sin finally came out with a despicable act.

When Joseph finally reached his brothers, he saw something fierce in their eyes. "Boy, am I glad I finally found you guys," he probably stated. But that gladness quickly changed to fear. The brothers assaulted him, tearing at the precious coat he wore, ripping it off of him.

"Stop! Leave my coat alone! What are you doing?" Can you imagine the scene? Perhaps two or three of them assaulted the young brother while the others stood around and watched with pleasure, like lion cubs watching their mother tear into her victim.

They cast Joseph into a pit, although the Bible doesn't say where this pit was located. Perhaps it was close by since they conversed about it as Joseph approached. They brutally threw him in. Most likely it was an empty well because the Bible tells us there was no water in it.

The brothers took Joseph's most prized possession from him, the coat of many colors. They hated that coat, a statement of their father's love and favoritism for a young man they despised. Rejection is never content just to do harm—it must also steal.

How sad that we live in a world where many young children are cast into pits. Sometimes an abusive father casts a child into a pit, or an overbearing mother does the job. Sometimes it is the cruelty of siblings that do it because of hatred against the child who is favored over them. Whatever the case, rejection will eventually climax in a terrible act, stealing something precious to the victim while casting him into the pit. Many times pride, hopes, and dreams are stolen, stripped off the victim just before the final push into a pit of despair.

The Pain of Rejection

Joseph begged his brothers to get him out, but they just laughed at him and sat down to eat. Imagine what Joseph was thinking as he sat in the pit. Thoughts of fear and hopelessness arose in his mind. He didn't know what his cruel brothers might do next. To them, he was worthless, and he probably felt like it. He was hated and despised. But more than anything, Joseph felt pain—deep, emotional pain. This kind of pain is the worst of all. He had been unjustly beaten and rejected.

What pain rejection can inflict! A simple word of rejection from a father or mother can cause deep, emotional pain in the heart of a child. Many times those biting words are far more painful than physical abuse. The pain of the physical abuse will eventually end, but those painful words will linger in the heart. While Joseph sat in the pit, no doubt the words of his brothers came to his mind. They had mocked him, called him names, and outright rejected him for his dreams.

Let me ask you, reader, are you experiencing the pain of rejection? Has a father, mother, brother, sister, friend, or leader rejected you unjustly? Have they hurt you with biting words? Have they taken your dreams and dashed them to pieces? Are you sitting in a pit of despair while they hover over you in triumph? It seems like there's nothing you can do.

Joseph couldn't do anything to get out of

that pit. As he sat there, he heard something in the distance. A caravan traveled by, and Judah had an idea. "Look, brothers! Here come some Ishmaelite merchants. We don't have to kill Joseph. Let's just sell him to these men." They all agreed this would be the best thing to do. So they pulled Joseph out of the pit and sold him for twenty pieces of silver. With that, the Ishmaelites carted Joseph to Egypt.

Now imagine what Joseph was thinking. He was sold by his own brothers and would now leave his homeland to live as a slave in a foreign land. A slave! That is what he was to his brothers. With big grins, the brothers probably waved at Joseph as he left. They were sure they would never see him again.

All of this took place because Reuben was not around for some reason. The Bible tells us that Reuben returned to the pit and discovered that Joseph was missing (vs. 29). "Oh, the dreamer?" the brothers asked. "We sold him to some Ishmaelite merchants. They took him off to Egypt." Reuben was devastated. He felt responsible for Joseph, and now he was gone. To conceal their evil deed, the brothers took Joseph's coat and dipped it in blood, presenting it to Jacob. Poor Jacob was easily convinced that a wild animal had killed his favorite son. In his mind, Joseph was dead.

Joseph's day had started like any other, but it had ended in complete despair. Now he was on his way to Egypt as a slave, and there was nothing he could do. Realize that when rejection hits you, there is nothing you can do. But it's wonderful to know there is a Sovereign God who can do anything *He* wants to do.

You Are Not Alone

Fred loved to sing and pursued his dream of being a singer. But at his first screen test at MGM, the testing director rejected him. He noted that Fred "can't act. Can't sing. Slightly bald. Can dance a little." Instead of giving up, Fred tried harder, and eventually acted in several films. Soon Fred Astaire was a star, making thirty-one musical films and several award-winning television specials.

Steve wanted to get into the movie business. He loved the power of movies and wanted to be able to direct and produce his own. He eagerly followed his dream, but was turned down three times by the University of Southern California School of Theater, Film and Television. He didn't give up though, and earned his BA to finally direct his own movies. Steven Spielberg went on to become one of the greatest film directors of all time, directing world-renowned movies such as E.T. the Extra-Terrestrial (1982) and Jurassic Park (1993).

Mike wanted to be a basketball player, but was cut from his high school basketball team for a "lack of skill." He went home and cried in the privacy of his room, but this did not stop him from playing the game. He picked himself back up and practiced constantly. He was accepted into the NBA by the Chicago Bulls, and Michael Jordan went on to become the greatest basketball player America has ever seen.

Walter was fired by his newspaper editor because he had no imagination and lacked any good ideas, so he set out to make his own company. It was not easy. Four times he had to deal with bankruptcy, but Walt Disney persisted and founded the Disney company. He is regarded as a cultural icon known for his leadership in the entertainment industry during the 20th century.

Perhaps you're thinking that these people persisted in their ways because they held onto their dreams. Perhaps your rejection comes not because of your dreams, but simply because of who you are. Is there anyone who can relate to this?

There was another person who was rejected, not because of His dreams, but because of who He was. Jesus, the Son of God, was rejected. Isaiah 53:3 tells us, *"He is despised and rejected of men…"* Even worse, we are told in John's gospel, *"He came unto his own, and his own received him not"* (John 1:11). His own people rejected Him! The Jews did not want Him as their Messiah, so they crucified Him. Jesus understands the rejection you are facing. He was persecuted, hated, and despised. Why was He rejected? Because He claimed to be the Son of God. The worst kind of rejection is the kind you experience because of who you are. Others envy you and therefore hate you. In such a case, you have to learn to get past the rejection.

Don't Let Rejection Stop You

The important thing to know is that God accepts you. God will never reject you. David made a strong statement in Psalm 27:10: *"When my father and my mother forsake me, then the LORD will take me up."* If your own family has rejected you, your heavenly Father has not. Jesus, your Savior, lovingly says to you, *"I will never leave thee, nor forsake thee"* (Heb. 13:5b). Your family and friends may stop loving you, but God will always love you. *"For I am persuaded, that neither death, nor life, nor angels, nor principalities, nor powers, nor things present, nor things to come, Nor height, nor depth, nor any other creature, shall be able to separate us from the love of God, which is in Christ Jesus our Lord"* (Rom. 8:38-39).

Rejection can hurt so badly because we naturally want to be accepted. We want our family to accept us. We want our friends to accept us. We want the world to accept us. But the only real Person who matters in your acceptance is God, and He has accepted you. *"To the praise of the glory of his grace, wherein he hath made us accepted in the beloved"* (Eph. 1:6). If you have put your faith in Christ, then God has accepted you just as He has accepted His own Son. Not everyone will accept you. We want the world to accept us, but realize that the world will hate you because it hated Jesus (see John 15:18). If you are in Christ, you will take part in Christ's rejection (the world), but you will also take part in Christ's acceptance (God). And God is the One who matters.

Author Paula Hendricks said this about rejection: "Human rejection can be God's divine protection." This was true for Joseph, and it can certainly be true for you. That painful rejection may be the catalyst which God uses to protect you and one day lead you to where He wants you to be.

Joseph was rejected by his brothers, but he was accepted by God. Perhaps he thought it was all over as he traveled to Egypt, or perhaps he simply gave it to God and said, "You are sovereign, God. And I know you gave me these dreams. I have been rejected and sold, but I will continue to do what is right." Despite the circumstances, Joseph held tightly to his integrity. No matter the circumstances, be a man or woman of integrity.

"And the Midianites sold him into Egypt unto

Potiphar, an officer of Pharaoh's, and captain of the guard" (vs. 36). Everything was about to change for Joseph, but Joseph himself would not change.

Three
Joseph's Prosperity
His Testimony

"And his master saw that the LORD was with him, and that the LORD made all that he did to prosper in his hand."
Genesis 39:3

In the early twentieth century, the American historian Roger Babson visited the president of Argentina. While he was there, the president asked him a question. "You are a student of history. Will you please tell me why it is that South America, with her unlimited resources, and having been settled earlier than North America, has nevertheless made much slower progress in civilization and material prosperity?"

Babson decided to throw the question back to the president. "Mr. President, you evidently have studied this question yourself, and I would be interested to know your answer to it." The President replied that he thought the explanation lay in the fact that South America was settled by Spaniards who came seeking gold while North America was settled by pilgrims who came seeking God.

We live in a world consumed with finding prosperity, whether physical, material, or spiritual. Turn on the television and it won't be long before you see a commercial claiming that you can lose forty pounds in two weeks. Listen to the radio for only a few minutes and you'll hear how you can make tons of money by joining a certain business. The internet is full of ads that claim you can win loads of cash by working from home. Casinos are popular because people are greedy, and they want to find prosperity without doing any work.

But real prosperity is not found in casinos or on the internet. Real prosperity is found only in God's Word. God made this clear when he addressed Joshua and the nation of Israel: *"This book of the law shall not depart out of thy mouth; but thou shalt meditate therein day and night, that thou mayest observe to do according to all that is written therein:* **for then thou shalt make thy way prosperous,** *and then thou shalt have good success"* (Josh. 1:8, emphasis mine).

The President of Argentina was absolutely right. A nation that seeks God over gold will find better prosperity. *"Blessed is the nation whose God is the LORD…"* (Psa. 33:12a). The word "blessed" means "happy." Those who are living for God are truly happy. They don't need to pursue money or weight-loss programs. They have everything they need in their relationship with the Lord.

Joseph was a man of prosperity because he put his faith and trust in God. Joseph's prosperity can be attributed to his integrity. We find him prospering in the worst situations under the worst circumstances. First, Joseph was sold as a slave and brought into Egypt. But the Bible tells us, *"And the LORD was with Joseph, and he was a prosperous man…"* (Gen. 39:2a). Later, Joseph was falsely accused by Potiphar's wife and cast into prison, but the Bible adds again, *"The keeper of the prison looked not to any thing that was under his hand; because the LORD was with him, and that which he did, the LORD made it to prosper"* (Gen. 39:23).

Prosperity is not based on your circumstances. Many times the rich and wealthy are not prospering at all because their faith is in their money, which cannot bring them happiness. Often it is the poor but faith-filled who have the real prosperity. Don't let the world deceive you into believing that prosperity is found only in money. How foolish to pursue something so temporal and unsatisfying! Only God can give you real prosperity, as evidenced by Joseph's life. Let's look at three important facts of prosperity found in this passage.

Prosperity is Connected with God

The first fact is found in verse 2 of Genesis 39: *"And the LORD was with Joseph, and he was a prosperous man…"* We see this truth emphasized again at the end of the chapter after the incident with Potiphar's wife. Real prosperity does not come from your money, it comes from the Lord. Whoever God attaches Himself to, that person will prosper.

To illustrate, let's say there was a billionaire, and this billionaire had a son. We could say: "And the billionaire was with his son, and the son was a prosperous man." Do you see it? The son was prosperous not because he was in the family business, but because the father chose to attach himself to the son, to teach him and help him. God works the same way.

The nation of Israel prospered because God attached Himself to her. Many times in the Old Testament God said to Israel, "I will be your God." Israel did not choose God; God chose Israel and attached Himself to her, and Israel prospered as long as the people obeyed the Lord.

It is the same way in our New Testament age. Jesus said to the disciples, *"Ye have not chosen me, but I have chosen you, and ordained you, that ye should go and bring forth fruit, and that your fruit should remain: that whatsoever ye shall ask of the Father in my name, he may give it you"* (John 15:16). Jesus attached Himself to the disciples in order that they would prosper with spiritual fruit.

You cannot prosper without the Lord. The best prosperity, however, comes when God is attached to us and we are likewise attached to Him. This is what the Bible calls abiding in

Christ. *"Abide in me, and I in you. As the branch cannot bear fruit of itself, except it abide in the vine; no more can ye, except ye abide in me"* (John 15:4). Christ is already abiding in you if you are saved. The question is, are you abiding in Him? Have you made the Lord Jesus the complete environment for your very life? Prosperity is not found in money or a health program, it is found in a Person.

The Bible compares us to trees, and trees cannot prosper in a dry environment. Notice what the first Psalm has to say about this: *"And he shall be like a tree planted by the rivers of water, that bringeth forth his fruit in his season; his leaf also shall not wither;* **and whatsoever he doeth shall prosper***"* (Psa. 1:3, emphasis mine). This is in reference to the godly person who has planted his roots deeply into God's Word. The "whatsoever" can be anything, whether physical, emotional, financial, relational, or spiritual. If you are not prospering, then you must not be abiding in Christ.

I believe Joseph was abiding in his God. Despite the circumstances, he was putting his faith in God and in those dreams he had received from God. He did not understand why this was happening to him, but he decided to plant himself there in Egypt and be the best slave he could be. So Joseph prospered in anything he did, only because God was with him. You cannot prosper apart from the Lord.

Prosperity is a Good Testimony to Others

Notice the next fact we find in the passage: *"And his master saw that the LORD was with him, and that the LORD made all that he did to prosper in his hand"* (vs. 3). Joseph's prosperity was seen and understood. God does not give you prosperity so you can sit on it. He gives it for a reason, and that reason is so you can use it as a testimony to others.

Joseph must have made his religious beliefs known. He was not ashamed to speak of Jehovah God openly around others. Perhaps he told them about God's covenant with his fathers. Word spread and Potiphar heard about it. Then he watched Joseph as he worked, and he saw that the Lord was indeed with him. No doubt he could not understand how this young man, who had been ripped away from his family and homeland, could be so happy as a slave in a foreign land.

Has God blessed you beyond measure? If you're breathing, then He has! You have far more than you deserve. Perhaps God has blessed you with more than others in a certain area. Use your prosperity as a good testimony to those around you. Let them know that God has blessed you, not luck or chance.

The Christian R.C. Chapman was once asked how he was feeling. "I'm burdened this morning!" was his reply. His words were contradicted by his happy countenance, so the questioner exclaimed, "Are you really burdened, Mr. Chapman?"

"Yes, but it's a wonderful burden—it's an overabundance of blessings for which I cannot find enough time or words to express my gratitude!" Seeing the puzzled look on the face of his friend, Chapman added with a smile, "I am referring to Psalm 68:19, which fully describes my condition. In that verse the Father in heaven reminds us that He daily loads us with benefits."

When God has blessed you so you can say with the Psalmist, *"my cup runneth over"* (Psa. 23:5b), let those blessings spill over onto others.

God gives us loads of blessings! Those blessings lead to prosperity, and that prosperity should lead to our praise of God. Tell those around you about how wonderful the Lord is in your life. Use prosperity as a means of testimony.

Joseph's prosperity and testimony led to a promotion. *"And Joseph found grace in his sight, and he served him: and he made him overseer over his house, and all that he had he put into his hand"* (vs. 4). Joseph's personal prosperity led to secular prosperity as he became Potiphar's right-hand man.

Why is it that many Christians are afraid to admit to their employers that they are Christians? Perhaps they know that their boss does not like religion, but they need to realize that their prosperity is in God's hand, not the employer's hand. If you are living for the Lord, then your prosperity is far greater than theirs, so make it known that God is blessing your life. Use that prosperity as a means to witness to those around you, and God may bless you even more for it.

The Bible says, *"The king's favour is toward a wise servant"* (Pro. 14:35a). Potiphar saw that

Joseph was a wise man, a hard worker, and a God-fearing man. Joseph was entrusted with great favor as Potiphar set him over his house. He trusted him with all of his things. Christian, more times than not, when you are in favor with God, you will find favor with man.

Prosperity Should Affect Others

Not only do others see your prosperity, but sometimes they may even experience it for themselves. Notice what the next verse has to say: *"And it came to pass from the time that he had made him overseer in his house, and over all that he had, that the LORD blessed the Egyptian's house for Joseph's sake; and the blessing of the LORD was upon all that he had in the house, and in the field"* (vs. 5). As soon as Joseph was promoted, God began blessing Potiphar's house for Joseph's sake. Joseph's prosperity spilled over onto Potiphar and his business.

We see the same incident in Genesis 30, in which God blessed Laban's crops because Jacob was with him. Laban evidently saw this, causing him to beg Jacob to stay. Notice his words: *"And Laban said unto him, I pray thee, if I have found favour in thine eyes, tarry: for I have learned by experience that the LORD hath blessed me for thy sake"* (Gen. 30:27). Jacob's prosperity had affected Laban as well. This is an important life principle. Your prosperity (or your failure) will affect others.

Dad, this is why it's so important that you work hard and provide for your family. Your prosperity or lack thereof will directly affect your family. When God blesses you, He blesses the entire family. The same can be said for the mother, or the son, or the daughter. God's blessing in our lives often spills over onto others, and they can say with Laban that God has blessed them for your sake.

However, the opposite can also be true. Remember Lot? His foolish choices cost his entire family. His sons-in-law were killed in the destruction of Sodom. His wife was transformed into a pillar of salt. His daughters, the only survivors, committed incest with him to produce Israel's future enemies, the Ammonites and Moabites. His failure to discern what was best for his family brought destruction to it. Prosperity or failure, both will affect others in your life.

The sad truth is, Christians who live like Lot lose their potential to be a godly testimony to others. God rescued Lot from the destruction of Sodom, but God could not bless Lot with prosperity. We cannot show others how amazing our God is if we are failing to live for Him! Lot could not persuade his sons-in-law to leave with them—they thought he was joking. And if your life does not match your words, your testimony will simply be a joke to those around you.

Joseph had a godly and sincere testimony. Yes, he was a slave, but he was the most prosperous slave you ever saw. Potiphar quickly realized his business was booming because of Joseph's godliness and hard work. Whatever Joseph set out to do, God blessed it.

We tend to separate the spiritual from the physical and the daily routines. We go to church on Sunday, but the rest of the week is different because we're out in the real world. But the spiritual should affect your work in the real world! Don't separate the two, put them together. Don't leave your testimony at church, take it with you and let it push you to work for the Lord. *"And whatsoever ye do, do it heartily, as to the Lord, and not unto men"* (Col. 3:23). Don't look at your job as working for your boss, but as working for God Himself. Joseph's spiritual life affected everything else, and it is the same with us.

Do You Have What It Takes?

So let me ask you, are you prospering? Are your relationships prospering? Is your family prospering, your ministry prospering, your job prospering, your health prospering, your _____ prospering? (Fill in the blank yourself!) If not, what's the reason? What was Joseph's secret to his success? He was a godly man with integrity.

Integrity is the key. God always blesses men and women who have integrity. But not just any kind of integrity, godly integrity. The choices you make are based upon your relationship with God. We see this in Joseph's life, and we will see it clearly in the next chapter. Has your relationship with God affected your choices? Remember, prosperity is connected with God.

Do you have a testimony? It's sad and shameful that some Christians have absolutely no testimony. Their friends and co-workers have no idea that they're Christians. Perhaps you have no testimony because you are not prospering. You are just like everyone else. Ask God to help you become a man or woman of integrity. Take your relationship with God seriously, and let that affect every area of your life.

This passage ends with these words: *"And Joseph was a goodly person, and well favoured"* (vs. 6b). Can those words be said of you? Can others see that you are a goodly person? Can they see that God has blessed you? If not, then you are not prospering as God intended. *"[The godly man] shall be like a tree planted by the rivers of water, that bringeth forth his fruit in his season; his leaf also shall not wither; and whatsoever he doeth shall prosper"* (Psa. 1:3).

Four
Joseph's Plight
His Character

"And it came to pass after these things, that his master's wife cast her eyes upon Joseph; and she said, Lie with me. But he refused…"
Genesis 39:7-8a

The year was 1896, and Norman "Kid" McCoy was the welterweight boxing champion. He earned that title with brawn, brains, but also tricks. In one of his fights, McCoy found out his opponent was deaf. He decided he could use this knowledge to his advantage in the fight, so as they were nearing the end of the third round, McCoy stepped back and pointed to his opponent's corner, indicating that the bell had rung. When the deaf fighter turned his head, McCoy unloaded a powerful blow and knocked him out. It wasn't fair, but it was certainly effective.

When it comes to the battle of the Christian life, Satan doesn't always play fair. He knows you better than you know yourself, and he certainly knows your greatest weaknesses. He will deliver the knock-out blow when you least expect it.

For Joseph, life was finally good again. He had complete trust and favor with his master Potiphar and everyone liked him. He was prospering and enjoying life, even though he was a lowly slave. Days became weeks, and weeks became months, and Joseph continued to thrive in his duties.

But one day, Potiphar's wife started eyeing him, then she moved in and talked with him, then she started flirting with him. Everyone could see it. And why not? Joseph was a handsome young Hebrew, but to attract his master's wife? Joseph became uneasy. She must have been a very attractive woman, perhaps with a youthful appearance, beautiful eyes, a slender figure, and a charming air about her.

No doubt this was when Satan came and sat on Joseph's shoulder. "Listen, you've been away from home for a long time. You don't have a companion. You're lonely, aren't you? Spend some time with her. No one will have to know. You can find comfort with her." If Joseph were Reuben, he would have quickly given in to his flesh. If he were Judah, he would have easily succumbed to lust.

But Joseph had something unique that many of Jacob's sons lacked: *character.* "No," he said. "I will not do that! She is my master's wife." Out of all the men and women in the Bible, Joseph gave us the best example of what to do when temptation comes along. In fact, Genesis 39 may be the best chapter in the Bible on temptation.

Let's look at four important actions Joseph used to defeat temptation that we need to use in our lives as well.

Focus on What You Have, Not on What You Lack

Mrs. Potiphar, an attractive Egyptian woman, took a liking to young Joseph. She probably assumed that she could easily seduce him. So one day she caught him and bluntly commanded, "Lie with me" (vs. 7). This was it. Joseph had the opportunity, the motive, and the person with whom he could do something he had never done before.

Consider Joseph's condition: he was a Hebrew slave ripped from his homeland and family. He had no lover or wife, possibly no real friends. It would have been easy for him to justify this sin. "I've been through a lot. I deserve this!" Many look at sin in this way, something they deserve to indulge in. They try to excuse the sin by blaming their circumstances.

But Joseph did not succumb to such a typical trap. He stood his ground with an incredible answer. Look at the first part: *"Behold, my master wotteth not what is with me in the house, and he hath committed all that he hath to my hand; There is none greater in this house than I; neither hath he kept back any thing from me but thee, because thou art his wife…"* (vs. 8-9a). Joseph's answer was common sense. He stated the fact that his master had given him everything except his wife. Would it be right of him to take advantage of his master's wife when his master had been so good to him?

Here is the key when it comes to the mindset of temptation: Focus on what you have instead of what you lack. That was what Joseph did. "You don't understand, Mrs. Potiphar. I have been given *responsibility* over all these things. I have been given *trust* and *friendship*. I cannot give those up in order to indulge in this sin with you." Satan wanted Joseph to focus on what he lacked, which was companionship, love, and sex. That is how temptation works.

The devil works in the mind of the believer to make him discontent—he wants you to think about those worldly pleasures which you lack. He wants you to look at the world and say, "I want that too." He is so deceitful. "Christian, look at what you're missing. They are having so much fun." But the pleasure of sin only lasts for a season.

Christian, don't focus on what you lack, focus on what you have. And what do you have? Here's a few possible things: a relationship with Jesus Christ, a home in heaven, the perfect Word of God, a Bible-believing church you attend, godly friends, a great job, a wonderful family, the promises of God, and the blessings of God. Look at all the things you have! Don't let Satan fool you.

The Bible tells us to be content with what we have. *"But godliness with contentment is great gain"* (I Tim. 6:6). We gain the most when we are content with the little that we have. We are spiritually rich in Christ. We don't need all the doo-dads of this world. Let's be like Joseph and have a little common sense.

Include God in Your Temptation

Notice the second part of Joseph's response to Mrs. Potiphar. *"...how then can I do this great wickedness, and sin against God?"* (vs. 9b). What an amazing thing to say! After he stated his logical reason, Joseph moved on to include God in the temptation. To indulge in this act would be great wickedness in the sight of God. Joseph recognized two important truths: (1) this act would be great wickedness (fornication), and (2) this act would be a sin against God Himself.

Had Joseph been thinking selfishly, he would have quickly given in to strong temptation. But Joseph contemplated what God would think of it. When one stops to consider God in the midst of a temptation, he is more likely not to fall into it.

Jesus fought temptation with the same kind of spiritual fortitude. When tempted by the devil himself, Jesus included God and the holy Scriptures. For all three temptations, Jesus said, "It is written," and quoted Scripture (see Matthew 4). Although He was physically weak from fasting, Jesus was spiritually strong and prepared for temptation. He was not selfishly thinking of Himself, but was ready to include God in the temptation. By including Scripture in times of need, we are including the Lord Himself.

Every sin that we willingly commit is because we are being selfish. But if we are careful to include God in the temptation, we will most likely not fall. So let's consider these two truths which Joseph used.

First, recognize that this sin would be great wickedness in the sight of God. We tend to downplay our sins. "It's only a little white lie," some may say. But how does God see lying? *"Lying lips are abomination to the LORD…"* (Pro. 12:22a). God sees any kind of lying as abomination.

"It's okay to live with your girlfriend," says our culture. "After all, marriage is a big commitment. You need to test this relationship ahead of time by living together to see if you're compatible." This terrible sin has even crept into the lives of young Christians in our churches. What does God have to say about the matter? *"Marriage is honourable in all, and the bed undefiled: but whoremongers and adulterers God will judge"* (Heb. 13:4). God sees this act as fornication, and He will judge this sin.

I could go on and on. The Bible is clear that God hates all sin; in His eyes, all sin is "great wickedness." We need to see it as such. Those sins you enjoy, the ones you pull out every now and then to embrace, are abominations to a holy God. Open your spiritual eyes to see sin as God sees it. Come to the place where you see sin as "exceeding sinful" (Romans 7:13d). Once you do, it will be much more difficult to embrace it.

Secondly, realize that your sin is against God. This is another truth we often fail to consider. When we lie, we do so to a specific person or a group of people, but in actuality our lying is against God.

In Acts chapter 5, Ananias and Sapphira, a couple in the Early Church, decided to lie about the price of the land they were giving to the church. They stated they were giving all the money they had received in the sale, when in actuality they were withholding part of it for themselves. They were lying to the church. But notice what Peter tells Ananias. *"Whiles it remained, was it not thine own? and after it was sold, was it not in thine own power? why hast thou conceived this thing in thine heart?* **thou has not lied unto men, but unto God"** (Acts 5:4, emphasis mine).

Ananias was indeed lying to the church, but Peter cut right to the severity of this sin: he was lying to God! Upon hearing this, Ananias fell down dead. The same thing happened later to his wife. The next time someone tells you that lying is not a big deal, tell them the story of Ananias and Sapphira.

This is true not only of lying, but also with every other sin we commit. Each sin is against God Himself. David recognized this after he committed the sin of adultery with Bathsheba. *"Against thee, thee only, have I sinned, and done this evil in thy sight..."* (Psa. 51:4a). David admits that his sin was against God, not Bathsheba or Uriah. You may sin *with* someone or *against* someone, but ultimately, your sin is against a righteous God. In the midst of temptation, stop and consider that this sin is against God, and He takes it personally.

As long as we are being selfish, we will fall for the temptation every time. Be sure to include God in the temptation, and remember how your sin will affect Him as well as you.

Avoid the Temptation

Mrs. Potiphar was stubborn. She must have been a woman who always got what she wanted, being catered to and spoiled. She would not take no for an answer with Joseph. She would get the young Hebrew one way or another. Every day she talked to him and tried to persuade him. *"And it came to pass, as she spake to Joseph day by day, that he hearkened not unto her, to lie by her, or to be with her"* (vs. 10).

Joseph had showed her his determination not to do what she wanted, but now he was pestered by her constantly. So he did his best to avoid her. Here we have a wonderful rule when it comes to temptation: avoid it at all costs. If you see temptation coming, go the other way. If the opportunity arises to be tempted, shut down the opportunity.

Solomon gave his son some wise counsel in Proverbs concerning this very truth. *"Enter not into the path of the wicked, and go not in the way of evil men. Avoid it, pass not by it, turn from it, and pass away"* (Pro. 4:14-15). Solomon was saying that we must do everything we can to avoid this evil path. Don't even go near it! Stay as far away as possible.

This truth is clearly presented in the New Testament by the Apostle Paul. *"But put ye on the Lord Jesus Christ, and make not provision for the flesh, to fulfil the lusts thereof"* (Rom. 13:14). Don't create opportunities to fall into sin; rather, do everything you can to avoid the temptation.

For example, it would not be wise for a man who used to be an alcoholic to walk down the beer isle at the grocery store. He needs to avoid even looking at the beer so as not to fall into this old sin. A porn addict should not have access to a computer, or he should not be able to get on the internet, lest he succumb to the temptation to look at pornography. If procrastination is your problem, you need to make a list of duties to do for each day and stick to that list no matter what.

You know your greatest weaknesses. What sin do you struggle with? It is your responsibility to avoid that sin and be careful not to make provision by which you might fall. Stay as far away as you can. When it comes to sin, you can never be too careful.

If All Else Fails, Run

One day Joseph entered the house to fulfill some business, and no one else was inside. While he was there, who should show up but Mrs. Potiphar. I imagine she sweet-talked him at first. "Joseph, darling, no one else is here. Come on, no one will ever know about it." Joseph outright refused. As he turned to leave, she grabbed his coat and shouted, "Lie with me!" Joseph did the smartest thing any man could do in such a situation: he ran. She ripped his coat from him on the way out, but Joseph escaped unscathed. However, the wicked mind of that woman started to turn. If Joseph would not do what she wanted, she would see to it that he was punished.

Joseph may have lost his coat, but he kept his character. Throughout the Bible we read of men and women alike who *fell to temptation*, but Joseph is the prime example of one who *fled from temptation.* Running is the best thing you can do when you're tempted, which is reiterated for us in the New Testament. *"Flee fornication"* (I Cor. 6:18). *"Wherefore, my dearly beloved, flee from idolatry"* (I Cor. 10:14). *"But thou, O man of God, flee these things..."* (I Tim. 6:11). *"Flee also youthful lusts..."* (II Tim. 2:22). The Bible is clear on this subject.

When all else fails, run. When the safeguards you have set up are destroyed and that temptation makes its way into your life, run. Do not stay and fight it (you will lose). Do not try to reason with it (you cannot reason with sin). Just run away as Joseph did.

Pastor Jeff Strite tells a remarkable story in a sermon he gave about Joseph. The following story is sad, yet true and telling of our culture today.

A man wrote about his experience when his 13-year-old son's school announced a meeting to preview the new course in sexuality. Parents could examine the curriculum and take part in an actual lesson presented exactly as it would be given to the students.

"When I arrived at school, I was surprised to discover only about a dozen parents were there. As we waited for the presentation, I thumbed through page after page of instructions in the prevention of pregnancy or disease.

I found abstinence mentioned only in passing. When the teacher arrived with the school nurse, she asked if there were any questions. I asked why abstinence did not play a noticeable part in the material. What happened next was shocking. There was a great deal of laughter, and someone suggested that if I thought abstinence had any merit, I should go back to burying my head in the sand.

The teacher and nurse said nothing as I drowned in embarrassment. My mind had gone blank, and I could think of nothing to say.

The teacher explained to me the job of the school was to teach 'facts,' and the home was responsible for moral teaching. I sat in silence for the next twenty minutes as the course was explained. The other parents seemed to give their unqualified support for the materials.

"Donuts, at the back," announced the teacher during the break. "I'd like you to put on the name tags we have prepared – they're right by the donuts – and mingle with the other parents."

Everyone moved to the back of the room. As I watched them affixing their name tags and shaking hands, I sat deep in thought. I was ashamed that I had not been able to convince them to include a serious discussion of abstinence in the materials. I uttered a silent prayer for guidance.

My thoughts were interrupted by the teacher's hand on my shoulder.

'Won't you go and join the others, Mr. Layton?' The nurse smiled sweetly at me. 'The donuts are good.'

'Thank you, no,' I replied.

'Well, then, how about a name tag? I'm sure the others would like to meet you.'

'Somehow I doubt that,' I replied.

'Won't you please join them?' she coaxed.

Then I heard a still, small voice whisper, 'Don't go.' The instruction was unmistakable. 'Don't go!'

'I'll just wait here,' I said.

When the class was called back to order, the teacher looked around the long table and thanked everyone for putting on name tags. She ignored me. Then she said, 'Now we're going to give you the same lesson we'll be giving your children. Everyone please peel off your name tags.'

I watched in silence as the name tags came off. 'Now, then, on the back of one of the tags, I drew a tiny flower. Who has it, please?'

The gentleman across from me held it up. 'Here it is!'

'All right,' she said. 'The flower represents disease. Do you recall with whom you shook hands?'

He pointed to a couple of people. 'Very good,' she replied. 'The handshake in this case represents intimacy. So the two people you had contact with now have the disease.'

There was laughter and joking among the parents. The teacher continued, 'And whom did the two of you shake hands with?'

The point was well taken, and she explained how this lesson would show students how quickly disease is spread.

'Since we all shook hands, we all have the disease.'

It was then that I heard the still, small voice again. 'Speak now,' it said 'but be humble.'

I noted wryly the latter admonition, then rose from my chair. I apologized for any upset I might have caused earlier, congratulated the teacher on an excellent lesson that would impress the youth, and then concluded by saying I had only one small point

I wished to make.

'Not all of us were infected,' I said. 'One of us... abstained.'"

Sexual disease today is looked upon by our culture as something we should just accept. It takes real character to refuse such a notion and to do what Joseph did. Joseph was the one who abstained. When pressured by a beautiful woman, he simply said no. He was, above all else, a man of integrity.

The best thing you can do is simply live an open life of godly integrity. Chuck Swindoll states it like this: "Few things are more infectious than a godly lifestyle. The people you rub shoulders with everyday need that kind of challenge. Not prudish. Not preachy. Just cracker jack clean living. Just honest to goodness, bone-deep, non-hypocritical integrity."

The Cost of Character

With the coat in her hand, Mrs. Potiphar screamed for help. She became a drama queen as she made up a compelling tale to tell the guard. "That Hebrew slave has mocked me! He tried to lie with me, so I screamed, and then he ran out. He left his coat with me when he escaped." She was convincing. This was the second time a coat of Joseph's was used in deceit about him. She told her husband the same thing when he came home. So what did Potiphar do? He threw Joseph in prison.

Now think about this: if a slave was caught fornicating with his master's wife, the penalty for him was death, not prison. So why was Joseph not killed? It is very possible that Potiphar did not believe his wife (after all, he trusted Joseph), but to appease her, he took Joseph and had him thrown in prison. No doubt he knew the way his wife often acted with young men. Now I could be wrong; after all, the Bible says that his wrath was kindled (vs. 19). But there was no wiggle room here. If such an act was committed, that slave would be killed for sure. And Joseph was not even an Egyptian, he was a foreign slave! No doubt Potiphar thought, "He is my best servant. I cannot take his life." So he threw him into prison.

Suddenly, Joseph's life was in pieces again. He had been falsely accused and mistreated. Now he was in prison, of all places! Yet there was still hope for the young Hebrew. He may have lost his position and his trust, but he still had God. *"But the LORD was with Joseph, and shewed him mercy, and gave him favour in the sight of the keeper of the prison"* (vs. 21).

Joseph first was favored by the Lord because he had done the right thing; he had done the moral thing. Then he was favored by the jail keeper, who allowed him to be in charge of all the prisoners. And with this favor came prosperity, not because Joseph was such a likable guy, but because the Lord was with him (vs. 23). Thus, everything he did prospered. Christian, God can make your bleakest situations suddenly prosper. There is nothing too hard for God.

Favor and prosperity followed Joseph wherever he went, no matter the circumstances. This can only be attributed to the fact that he was a godly man of character, something which Jacob's other sons knew nothing about. But then again, they never experienced the fires of God's testing.

If you want to be a man or woman of integrity, it will cost you. Some will appreciate it, but others will despise it. You may be accused or jeered by some, but remember that God's blessings will surround you, even if your circumstances give way to seeming disaster. In the best of times and in the worst of times, your integrity will clearly be seen.

Five
Joseph's Predictions
His Compassion

"And they said unto him, We have dreamed a dream, and there is no interpreter of it. And Joseph said unto them, Do not interpretations belong to God? tell me them, I pray you."
Genesis 40:8

Joseph was seventeen years old when he entered Egypt as a lowly slave. We are not told how old he was when he was thrown in prison. Perhaps he had faithfully served Potiphar for three years before the temptation incident, so he would have been twenty years old when cast in the dungeon. If that was the case, he was in prison for ten long years, for the Bible tells us he was thirty when he was finally released (Gen. 41:46). Were those years a waste? Not in the least. Those years taught Joseph to wait on the Lord, trust in Him, and see Him work out all the details.

Joseph had been in prison now for quite some time. He was actually in charge of the prisoners because he had found favor in the sight of the jail keeper. One day, Pharaoh's butler and baker somehow offended Pharaoh, and they were both thrown into the prison.

I wonder what these two men had done. The butler was the Pharaoh's cupbearer; perhaps he tasted too much of the king's wine. "How dare you drink that much! Into the prison with you!" Probably not, but that's all I can think of. The baker obviously baked something to the king's disliking. "This bread tastes like concrete! My dead mummy relatives could make better bread! Into the prison!" So these two poor fellows were cast in prison. Joseph quickly showed them great kindness. He served them faithfully for a few months (vs. 4).

One night, both of these men dreamed his own dream. Remember back in that day, dreams were significant—they could mean something important to a person's life (unlike today, where dreams are usually produced because of late night snacking). The next morning, Joseph discerned that something was wrong with these men. "Why are you so sad today?" he asked. They told him that they both had dreams, but there was no one to interpret the dreams for them. Joseph realized that if anyone could interpret those dreams, it was God. And because Joseph was very close to the Lord, he was confident that He would reveal the truth of the dreams to him. "Interpretations belong to God, and I just happen to know Him. Come on, tell me your dreams."

The closer you are to the Lord, the better you will be at helping others. God blessed Joseph with a gift for dreams (both dreaming and interpreting). We also need to use our God-given gifts to help others. Joseph showed compassion on these men by taking the time to listen to them and help them understand what the dreams meant.

The Butler's Dream

The butler reluctantly told Joseph his dream. He was not sure if the young Hebrew could interpret it, but he had nothing to lose.

"And the chief butler told his dream to Joseph, and said to him, In my dream, behold, a vine was before me: and in the vine were three branches:

and it was as though it budded, and her blossoms shot forth; and the clusters thereof brought forth ripe grapes: And Pharaoh's cup was in my hand: and I took the grapes, and pressed them into Pharaoh's cup, and I gave the cup into Pharaoh's hand" (vs. 9-11).

This dream was indeed strange, but Joseph must have smiled immediately. He knew the outcome of this dream. *"And Joseph said unto him, This is the interpretation of it: The three branches are three days: Yet within three days shall Pharaoh lift up thine head, and restore thee unto thy place: and thou shalt deliver Pharaoh's cup into his hand, after the former manner when thou wast his butler"* (vs. 12-13).

This was good news for the butler, who went from nervous agitation to immediate relief and joy. Joseph's confidence no doubt gave him confidence that what he had said would come to pass. His lost position, which he thought he would never have again, would be reclaimed.

Then Joseph added a personal note. *"But think on me when it shall be well with thee, and shew kindness, I pray thee, unto me, and make mention of me unto Pharaoh, and bring me out of this house: For indeed I was stolen away out of the land of the Hebrews: and here also have I done nothing that they should put me into the dungeon"* (vs. 14-15).

Joseph realized that the butler could help him get out of the dungeon. I imagine the butler quickly nodded his head, saying, "Oh yes, my friend, I will tell them you're down here, and you will get out just like me." A huge smile must have filled his once gloomy face. Joseph had brought him hope again.

The Baker's Dream

Seeing the joy of the butler, the baker eagerly asked Joseph to interpret his dream as well. Surely he would also reclaim his former position.

"When the chief baker saw that the interpretation was good, he said unto Joseph, I also was in my dream, and, behold, I had three white baskets on my head: and in the uppermost basket there was of all manner of bakemeats for Pharaoh; and the birds did eat them out of the basket upon my head. And Joseph answered and said, This is the interpretation thereof: The three

baskets are three days: Yet within three days shall Pharaoh lift up thy head from off thee, and shall hang thee on a tree; and the birds shall eat thy flesh from off thee" (vs. 16-19).

The poor baker did not get the same answer as did the butler. Instead of reclaiming his former position, he would suffer an execution. Joseph must have somberly told him the news and tried to comfort him. I imagine Joseph practiced what Ephesians 4:15 says—he spoke the truth in love.

The butler anticipated being restored to his former position of cupbearer. The baker, on the other hand, dreaded his execution, fearing his life would soon be over. And Joseph must have encouraged them each day in whatever way he could. A man of integrity would do no less.

The Predictions Come True

The three days slowly went by. The butler and baker nervously waited, wondering if Joseph's predictions would happen as he said. Finally, the third day arrived. It was Pharaoh's birthday, so he decided to make a feast for all his servants. The prison door was flung open and the guard called for the butler and the baker. "Pharaoh wants to see you two." They looked at one another and slowly moved toward the door. As the door closed, Joseph knew that his predictions had come true, the predictions which God had given him.

That day, the butler was restored to his former position. He must have felt honored to serve Pharaoh once again. The baker, however, was hanged on that same day. Pharaoh did not deem him worthy of getting a second chance.

We should strive to help others and show them the love of Christ, but realize that not everyone you help will turn out for the better. Some will be gloriously restored, finding blessing and fulfillment in living for Christ. Others will try by their own power and be destroyed. Some will reject your help, rejecting the gospel you share, and will end up being hanged by their own decision. No matter the results, don't just give them advice, give them compassion.

Compassion Makes the Difference

George Truett was a tremendously effective pastor for decades in Texas. His heart was broken when he accidentally killed his best friend while they were on a hunting trip. His daughter said she never heard him laugh after that day. Truett had a radio program, and each day when it came to a close he would say, "Be good to everybody, because everybody is having a tough time." He knew personally what a heavy burden people could be carrying, and he encouraged compassion toward everyone.

This was the case with the butler and the baker. They both had heavy hearts after what recently happened to them, and the dreams only added to the weight. By simply listening to their problems, Joseph showed them compassion, but he went a step further and helped them.

Jude 22 gives us a simple truth: *"And of some have compassion, making a difference."* When you see someone with a heavy heart, take time to listen to their problem (many do not even do that), and then find a way to help and encourage them. Joseph was able to interpret their dreams, and in his position, that was all he could do. But you can do far more than that.

Usually when someone tells us about a problem, we respond by saying, "I'll pray for you." That's good, but what else can you do for them? Many times we say that without even thinking, as if it's a spiritual reflex. The sad truth is, many times there is no compassion behind those words. Theologian Francis Schaeffer said, "Biblical orthodoxy without compassion is surely the ugliest thing in the world."

Real compassion is seen in action, not words. This is what John wanted Christians to understand when he said, *"My little children, let us not love in word, neither in tongue; but in deed and in truth"* (I John 3:18). Love is never content to just speak—it must reach out in some way and perform action.

When I was a sophomore in college, my grandmother passed away. She was in perfect health, so it came as a shock to my family. It was especially hard for me because I had never lost a close family member before. My roommate and best friend was there when I received the news over the phone. He did not just tell me he would pray for me, he got down on his knees and prayed *with* me. He showed me compassion during a difficult time, and I am ever grateful for that.

Ask yourself, what can I do for this person?

Perhaps a close friend's relative has passed away; spend time with them and pray with them. Perhaps someone you love has cancer; once again, spend time with them. Perhaps someone you know is struggling with an addiction; find a way to encourage them and help them overcome their addiction.

John Bunyan understood compassion when he said, "You have not lived today until you have done something for someone who can never repay you." Words are not enough. Real compassion and real love always produce action, and a man of integrity is a man of compassion.

Six
Joseph's Patience
His Waiting

"Yet did not the chief butler remember Joseph, but forgat him."
Genesis 40:23

Whether we realize it or not, we wait on several things every day. We wait in traffic on the way to work. We wait for the microwave while our food is heating. We wait for our children to come home from school. We wait in line at the grocery store. The fact is, waiting is a big part of our lives.

Did you know that waiting is also a big part of the Christian life? If we cannot learn to wait on the Lord, then we will stay immature Christians. But if we can master waiting, then we have mastered one of the greatest principles in life.

Joseph learned to wait. As I mentioned before, let's say he was cast into prison at age twenty. According to Genesis 41:1, two full years went by after the butler and baker were released. The Bible also tells us that Joseph was thirty years old when he got out (Gen. 41:46), meaning that he possibly had been in prison for eight years when the butler was released. He hoped to get out, thanks to the butler, but then waited another two years. That's ten years! Ten years of waiting on the Lord to fulfill His promises.

Yet we never read of Joseph complaining. The only verse we read for these years of waiting is the last verse of chapter 40, which states that the butler forgot about Joseph when he was restored.

Waiting is very important in the Christian life. This word "wait" means "to look for, to expect." H. Richard Hester describes this word as follows: "The word has the concept of to twist or bind as one twists together the strands to make a rope. Maybe 'wait' is taking the strands of visible blessing and knowledge of the Lord and His goodness, and twisting them all together into a strong rope of confidence that breeds hope and expectation."

This kind of waiting is not like waiting at the

doctor's office; that is more of a dreadful waiting. This is the kind of waiting that a child does when he is excited to open his Christmas presents—*it is an expected waiting*. God wants to work in our lives, but there are times when we must wait for Him to work. And during those times, God wants to grow us and teach us. These times are important! The gift would not mean much if we did not have to wait to receive it.

We live in a fast-paced culture. With just one touch, we can instantly look at several internet pages at once. Fast-food restaurants pride themselves on getting our food to us as quickly as possible. Automobile manufacturers do their best to max out their cars with the highest top speed. Yet amid such a fast-paced culture, God wants us to slow down and learn to wait. God always makes us wait for the things we want the most. The Bible has a lot to say about waiting, so it's obviously important.

You might be like me: very impatient. How does God's Word prove that we need to wait? Let's look at four main reasons from the Bible why patience is vital to the Christian life.

Patience Produces Strength

It's hard to wait on the Lord when you don't see anything happening. It can be easy to think, "Does God really care? Is He really working in my life?" But God promises that in those times, He will give you strength. Psalm 27:14 tells us, *"Wait on the LORD: be of good courage, and he shall strengthen thine heart: wait, I say, on the LORD."* When the heart is doubting, the Bible says God will strengthen it. I imagine Joseph had some doubts while sitting in the dungeon, but I also believe he found strength in the Lord.

The heart in the Bible always refers to the mind, will, and emotions. When we are impatient, we often lose control of our mind, will, and emotions. We begin to doubt God. We say things that are hopeless. We become emotional and find ourselves in fits of rage or tears. We need to ask God for strength to wait.

The Bible tells us that our strength can be renewed. *"But they that wait upon the LORD shall renew their strength; they shall mount up with wings as eagles; they shall run, and not be weary; and they shall walk, and not faint"* (Isa.

40:31). Eagles have strong wings. They flap their wings to gain speed and altitude, then they soar on the wind. While they're soaring and gliding, they are able to renew their strength. This is how God wants to work in your life. When we believe God by faith, we are flapping our wings, and then we must wait on the Lord to do what we are trusting Him for. That is when our strength is renewed.

Patience Produces Hope

When we have to wait for long periods of time, we can easily become depressed and have a hopeless attitude. God knew this, which is why He promises to give us hope in times of waiting. Notice what this Psalm has to say:

Out of the depths have I cried unto thee, O LORD. Lord, hear my voice: let thine ears be attentive to the voice of my supplications. If thou, LORD, shouldest mark iniquities, O Lord, who shall stand? But there is forgiveness with thee, that thou mayest be feared.

I wait for the LORD, my soul doth wait, and in his word do I hope. My soul waiteth for the Lord more than they that watch for the morning: I say, more than they that watch for the morning.

Let Israel hope in the LORD: for with the LORD there is mercy, and with him is plenteous redemption.

And he shall redeem Israel from all his iniquities.
Psalm 130:1-8

Hope is expectation. "My soul doth wait, and in his word do I hope." We see here that waiting and hoping are connected. This is true of many events in life: waiting for a birthday party, waiting for Christmas, or waiting for an important job interview. During these times of waiting, we are hopeful for that event; we are expecting something good to happen.

Notice this phrase from verse 6, "My soul waiteth for the Lord more than they that watch for the morning." The morning is expected to come. We set our alarm clocks because we expect morning to come, and we are not surprised when it arrives. Our waiting on the Lord should be more expectant than our expectation that the sun will rise and the morning will come.

Why would we look forward to Christmas if we didn't believe it would ever come? What's the point? A child is willing to wait for Christmas because he knows it will arrive. Do you believe God will work in your life? Then wait and hope in the Lord. Have an eager expectation for what He will do.

John Piper points out the importance of waiting and hoping in the Lord: "To wait on God means to pause and soberly consider our own inadequacy and the Lord's all-sufficiency, and to seek counsel and help from the Lord, and to hope in Him (Ps. 33:20-22; Isa. 8:17) … The folly of not waiting for God is that we forfeit the blessing of having God work for us. The evil of not waiting on God is that we oppose God's will to exalt Himself in mercy."

Patience Produces a Perfect Work

Patience can produce something that nothing else can. But if you want it, you're going to have to go through some trials. We find this truth in the book of James. *"My brethren, count it all joy when ye fall into divers temptations; Knowing this, that the trying of your faith worketh patience. But let patience have her perfect work, that ye may be perfect and entire, wanting nothing"* (Jam. 1:2-4).

This passage is in the context of trials. Honestly, simply waiting on God can be a trial. So what is this perfect work? It is spiritual maturity.

If you let patience work in your life, you will be perfect (that is, mature), entire (complete), and wanting (or lacking) nothing. That sounds pretty good! In other words, you will be a spiritually mature Christian who is living a fulfilling and enriching life. There will be no holes in your life, and all of your needs will be met.

However, should you refuse to let patience work in your life, you will become immature, incomplete, and lacking in life. Sadly, many Christians are living this way because they are not willing to wait on the Lord. Instead of waiting for the right spouse, many singles have married worldly believers or even non-believers and are now incomplete, being out of God's perfect will for their lives.

Rushing ahead of God will only make us immature, like a spoiled child who gets everything he wants. God does not spoil us, but He allows the consequences of our decisions to play out, and many times they leave us unhappy and unfulfilled. Don't blame God for bad decisions you made in your life. You need to let patience work.

Patience Leads to Godliness

Patience is one of the many qualities in the Christian life, which is important in the process of Christian living. "Biblically, waiting is not just something we have to do until we get what we want. Waiting is part of the process of becoming what God wants us to be" (John Ortberg).

How important is it to wait? Notice these verses from the book of II Peter: *"And beside this, giving all diligence, add to your faith virtue; and to virtue knowledge; And to knowledge temperance; and to temperance patience; and to patience godliness"* (II Pet. 1:5-6).

These are stages of spiritual growth. The very first stage is faith, that is, saving faith. Once you are saved, the next stage is virtue. The Greek word is *arete*, which means "manliness, excellence, more specifically, moral vigor." In other words, it's time to become a man. Every Christian needs to have moral vigor, a strong stance for morality.

The third stage is knowledge. This has to do with moral wisdom, such as is seen in right living. You stand for morality, but now you need to live it. The next stage is where many Christians fail: temperance or self-control. This can be a difficult quality in the culture in which we live. Our culture constantly tells us to buy things and make ourselves happy. But with the help of the Holy Spirit, we can live lives of self-control and self-discipline.

If you thought that was a hard stage, the next one is the hardest of all: patience. To fully understand, we need to look at its Greek word *hupomone,* which means "steadfastness, constancy, endurance; the characteristic of a man who is unswerved from his deliberate purpose and his loyalty to faith and piety by even the greatest trials and sufferings."

We see here that patience is truly an incredible characteristic to have! Patience can only be created in your life by trials and testing. The person who has never faced trials has no idea what patience is because it can only be developed in the fires of testing. Do you want patience? It will not be easy to obtain, and indeed many never acquire it.

But you certainly want patience because it leads to the best stage of all: godliness! This is holiness, the desire to live a godly life. Without patience, you are not a godly Christian, you are an immature one. This is why patience is so important, and this is why Joseph was able to become an amazing man of God. You cannot be a man of integrity without patience.

Waiting is a Choice

In 1970, Walter Mischel and Ebbe B. Ebbesen conducted the first "Marshmallow Test" at Stanford University. Children ages four to six were used as test subjects. The child was led into a room containing only a table with one marshmallow resting on the table. He could choose to eat the marshmallow immediately or wait for fifteen minutes in order to get a second marshmallow. During the fifteen minutes, the worker would leave the room, leaving the child alone.

Mischel observes that some would "cover their eyes with their hands or turn around so that they can't see the tray, others start kicking the desk, or tug on their pigtails, or stroke the marshmallow as if it were a tiny stuffed animal," while others would simply eat the marshmallow as soon as the researchers left. The younger children were the ones who tended to eat the first marshmallow; the older ones were able to wait.

As the years went on, the test results proved that those who had waited were more responsible and were able to make better decisions in times of crisis. Those who had not waited proved to be more immature and fickle in times of decision.

Charles Spurgeon, the Prince of Preachers, sums it up well: "If the Lord Jehovah makes us wait, let us do so with our whole hearts; for blessed are all they that wait for Him. He is worth waiting for. The waiting itself is beneficial to us: it tries faith, exercises patience, trains submission, and endears the blessing when it comes. The Lord's people have always been a waiting people."

Christian, is God making you wait for something in your life? You must choose whether to wait on the Lord or to gratify yourself now. But remember, if you wait, the results will be far better. Make Micah 7:7 your personal plea: *"Therefore I will look unto the LORD; I will wait for the God of my salvation: my God will hear me."* Make the right choice. Be willing to say "I will wait for God."

Imagine what would have happened if Joseph had not been willing to wait. He would have become angry and bitter. He would have taken matters into his own hands. He would have ruined everything. When we wait, we allow God to work everything out in His own time.

Those who learn to wait master one of life's greatest difficulties. It takes a man of integrity to wait for God's plan to unfold.

Seven
Joseph's Puzzle
His Faith

"And Joseph said unto Pharaoh, The dream of Pharaoh is one: God hath shewed Pharaoh what he is about to do."
Genesis 41:25

One night Pharaoh laid down to sleep, not realizing what awaited him. He had two dreams that night, and they were as clear as day. These were not hazy dreams which we so often have. They were crystal clear, for God had a message in them.

In the first dream, Pharaoh saw seven healthy cows come up out of the Nile River. They were fat and pleasant, the kind of cows any farmer would want. But then seven other cows came up. They were skinny to the bone and looked like they would fall over with disease. These awful cows turned on the healthy ones and ate them up. Pharaoh awoke. What a horrible dream!

He went back to sleep and had another dream. This time he saw seven ears of corn, all of them shining with great radiance, the kind of corn that propels a nation into wealth. But then seven more ears of corn appeared, and these were wretched! They were spotted and rotting. These bad ears devoured the seven ears of ripe corn. Pharaoh woke up with a jolt! "That's my corn, you—" But it was just a dream.

Pharaoh realized these dreams were connected, and they had to mean something. So he assembled all his wise men and magicians. *"...and Pharaoh told them his dream; but there was none that could interpret them unto Pharaoh"* (Gen. 41:8b).

Pharaoh was frustrated. "If only we had someone who could interpret dreams." The butler was standing by and suddenly remembered. Of course! Two years ago, when he was in prison, there was a young Hebrew man who had perfectly interpreted his dream (and the poor Baker's dream too). What was the man's name? He could not remember, but he was confident that he could interpret Pharaoh's dream.

"Oh, your Greatness, when the baker and I were in prison, we both had dreams. There was a young Hebrew there who interpreted our dreams, and they came true just as he had said!" Pharaoh was intrigued to hear this, and sent for this young man.

Meanwhile, Joseph was doing the menial tasks which he had been given to do. Perhaps he was chatting with some prisoners or scrubbing the floors, when all of a sudden, an Egyptian guard rushed up to him. "Joseph, you have been summoned by Pharaoh!"

"Pharaoh wants to see me?" asked Joseph. "Why?"

The guard grabbed him. "I don't know, but you must change into something presentable and shave. Quickly now!"

The day had finally come. All of the years of waiting and suffering were over. Joseph was about to be propelled into the greatest years of his life. Everything was about to change. No longer would he live in obscurity; soon he would be living in the years of opportunity.

With great reverence, Joseph approached Pharaoh. *"And Pharaoh said unto Joseph, I have dreamed a dream, and there is none that can interpret it: and I have heard say of thee, that thou canst understand a dream to interpret it"* (vs. 15). This was Joseph's big chance. God had given him an opportunity to use his greatest gift and to display his faith in Jehovah God.

Satan must have tempted him in that moment. "Don't you dare mention your God. Pharaoh would be insulted; after all, the Egyptians treat him as an incarnate god himself. Don't blow it now, Joseph. Take pride in yourself and leave God out of it." But Joseph had not gone through all of God's testings and trials just to fail. This young man never missed an opportunity to witness for his God, whether it was in front of Potiphar, or his wicked wife, or in front of Pharaoh himself.

Faith is a huge part of the Christian life. We are nothing, and can do nothing, without faith in God. Here we see Joseph's unwavering faith displayed in his all-knowing God. He had quite a puzzle on his hands, but he had confidence that God would solve it. Let's notice three important keys to faith.

Faith Knows that God will Work

Pharaoh explained his dilemma to young Joseph. He had a dream, and no one was able to tell him what it meant. When he acknowledged Joseph's special ability to interpret dreams, Joseph responded with a faith-filled answer. *"And Joseph answered Pharaoh, saying, It is not in me: God shall give Pharaoh an answer of peace"* (vs. 16).

We see two simple truths in this verse. First, Joseph recognized that he could not do it on his own, and secondly, Joseph was confident that God would give an answer. Joseph was not worried. He had seen dreams fulfilled which God had allowed him to interpret, and he knew that God could do it again.

Christian, recognize first that you cannot do it on your own. When we make this mistake, we are setting ourselves up to fail. Moses was afraid to confront Pharaoh, but God assured him that He would be with him. When he stated that he could not speak, God said, *"Now therefore go, and I will be with thy mouth, and teach thee what thou shalt say"* (Ex. 4:12).

Joshua must have been greatly afraid about leading the children of Israel, but God assured him that he would not be alone. *"Have not I commanded thee? Be strong and of a good courage; be not afraid, neither be thou dismayed:* ***for the LORD thy God is with thee whithersoever thou goest"*** (Josh. 1:9, emphasis mine). God was with Joshua every step of the way.

Moses and Joshua could not do it on their own. They knew this, and so did the Lord. God often calls us to do things that are beyond our abilities. He does this to show us that we need Him and we must depend on Him. We need to say as Joseph said, "It is not in me."

Secondly, put your confidence in God for the answer. Joseph was counting on God to interpret the dream of Pharaoh. This was a big deal! It was a make-or-break moment, and Joseph's future depended on it.

Christian, God will cause you to wait in order to prepare you for that big moment. He wants to make sure you're ready. When it comes, don't blow it. Be ready to put all your confidence in the Lord for the answer. The very middle verses of the Bible tell us this: *"It is better to trust in the LORD than to put confidence in man. It is better to trust in the LORD than to put confidence in princes"* (Psa. 118:8-9).

George Mueller knew how to put confidence in God for the answer. He started many orphanages in England in the 1800s and learned to trust God to provide for all their needs.

One morning, he and the orphans gathered around the table for breakfast, but all the plates, bowls, and cups were empty. There was no food in the kitchen. Mueller looked at the children and said, "Children, you know we must be in time for school." Then lifting up his hands he prayed, "Dear Father, we thank Thee for what Thou art going to give us to eat."

There was a knock at the door. It was the baker, who said, "Mr. Mueller, I couldn't sleep last night. Somehow I felt you didn't have bread for breakfast, and the Lord wanted me to send you some. So I got up at 2 a.m. and baked some fresh bread, and have brought it."

Mr. Mueller thanked the baker, and shortly after he left there was another knock at the door. It was the milkman. He stated that his milk cart had broken down right in front of the orphanage, and he wanted to give the children his cans of fresh milk so they would not spoil.

God will answer your request of faith! In those times when you need Him most, put your confidence in God. He will never fail you. Faith knows that God will work.

Faith Always Gets an Answer

With Joseph giving his undivided attention, Pharaoh related his dreams. He told how the seven starving cows ate up the seven healthy ones. He repeated about the seven ears of withered corn eating up the seven ears of good corn. Then he asked, "What does it all mean?"

Joseph didn't miss a beat. *"And Joseph said unto Pharaoh, The dream of Pharaoh is one: God hath shewed Pharaoh what he is about to do"* (vs. 25). And he goes on to explain what the dream means.

The seven good kine are seven years; and the seven good ears are seven years: the dream is one. And the seven thin and ill favoured kine that came up after them are seven years; and the seven empty ears blasted with the east wind shall be seven years of famine.

This is the thing which I have spoken unto Pharaoh: What God is about to do he sheweth unto Pharaoh. Behold, there come seven years of great plenty throughout all the land of Egypt: And there shall arise after them seven years of famine; and all the plenty shall be forgotten in the land of Egypt; and the famine shall consume the land; And the plenty shall not be known in the land by reason of that famine following; for it shall be very grievous. And for that the dream was doubled unto Pharaoh twice; it is because the thing is established by God, and God will shortly bring it to pass.

Genesis 41:26-32

God revealed to Joseph the meaning of the dream. Joseph's confidence in God's power to reveal the dream was not misguided or rash, it was true. Here we see that faith always gets an answer.

It was Jesus who said, *"Therefore I say unto you, What things soever ye desire, when ye pray, believe that ye receive them, and ye shall have them"* (Mark 11:24). Faith is the key in getting answers to our prayers. This was true in the lives of many Bible characters.

Abraham was commanded by God to sacrifice his only son. It seemed insane, yet Abraham put his faith in God. He believed God would continue his seed through his son Isaac, so much so that he thought God would raise Isaac from the dead (see Heb. 11:19). Abraham passed the test, and God provided a ram instead of his son.

In the contest on Mount Carmel, Elijah was confident that God would answer by fire and prove to all the Baal worshipers that He was the true God. His faith received an answer: fire from heaven, which consumed the sacrifice and licked up all the water (see I Sam. 18:36-39).

The three young Hebrews put their faith and trust in the Lord when threatened to be cast into the fiery furnace. Their response to King Nebuchadnezzar was one of great faith: *"If it be so, our God whom we serve is able to deliver us from the burning fiery furnace, and he will deliver us out of thine hand, O king. But if not, be it known unto thee, O king, that we will not serve thy gods, nor worship the golden image which thou hast set up"* (Dan. 3:17-18). And their faith received an answer as God miraculously delivered them.

If anything moves God to action, it is faith. It can be easy to fall into the trap of thinking that God does not reward faith today like He did in Bible times, but there are many contemporary accounts as well.

For ten years, missionaries Robert and Mary Moffat labored faithfully in Bechuanaland (now called Botswana) without a single convert. The directors of their mission board began to question if they should allow them to continue the work. But the young couple were grieved to think of leaving their work, believing God would eventually bless their labors. So they stayed.

Then one day a friend in England sent word to the Moffats that she wanted to mail them a gift and asked what they would like. Trusting that in time the Lord would bless their work, Mrs. Moffat replied, "Send us a communion set; I am sure it will soon be needed." God honored her faith, and within a short time six souls were saved and united to form the first Christian church in that land. The communion set arrived in the mail the day before the first Lord's Supper service.

When Hudson Taylor went to China, he made

the voyage on a sailing vessel. As it neared the channel between the southern Malay Peninsula and the island of Sumatra, the missionary heard an urgent knock on his stateroom door.

It was the captain of the ship. "Mr. Taylor," he said, "we have no wind. We are drifting toward an island where the people are heathen, and I fear they are cannibals."

"What can I do?" asked Taylor.

"I understand that you believe in God. Please pray for wind."

"All right, Captain, I will, but you must set the sail."

"Why that's ridiculous! There's not even the slightest breeze. Besides, the sailors will think I'm crazy."

But finally, because of Taylor's insistence, he agreed. Forty-five minutes later he returned and found the missionary still on his knees. "You can stop praying now," said the captain. "We've got more wind than we know what to do with!"

A man named Sam tells a personal answer to prayer. "Years ago, I heard a sermon where our pastor read a scripture that says, 'he who does not repay a debt is brother of him who steals.' I felt very guilty because I owed my brother $50, but I had put it off and didn't have the cash on hand. The next morning I prayed that God would provide the money to pay my brother back. An hour later I went to check my mail and there was a check for $50 from a long distance company stating that if I wanted to switch service to just sign and deposit the check that was addressed to me! So, I was able to pay my brother back and got a great deal on long distance service, too."

People have put their faith in God to see others healed of cancer, lost friends saved, see God provide for their needs, and witnessed personal requests answered just in time.

We can be confident that God responds to faith because of what the Bible tells us. *"For verily I say unto you, That whosoever shall say unto this mountain, Be thou removed, and be that cast into the sea; and shall not doubt in his heart, but shall believe that those things which he saith shall come to pass; he shall have whatsoever he saith"* (Mark 11:23). When the woman with the blood disease touched Jesus, the Savior told her this: *"Daughter, be of good comfort; thy faith hath made thee whole"* (Matt. 9:22), and she was healed. Remember that we are putting our faith in God, and Luke 1:37 states, *"For with God nothing shall be impossible."*

How important is faith! Rest assured, Christian, that faith always receives an answer from the Lord, and it is always the answer you need at just the time you need it. Andrew Murray said it best: "Faith expects from God what is beyond all expectation."

Faith is Always Rewarded

After Joseph explained the dream about seven years of plenty followed by seven years of famine, he gave this advice:

Let Pharaoh do this, and let him appoint officers over the land, and take up the fifth part of the land of Egypt in the seven plenteous years. And let them gather all the food of those good years that come, and lay up corn under the hand of Pharaoh, and let them keep food in the cities. And that food shall be for store to the land against the seven years of famine, which shall be in the land of Egypt; that the land perish not through the famine.

Genesis 41:34-36

Joseph knew they must take advantage of the seven years of plenty if they were to survive during the seven years of famine. "Pharaoh, you should appoint someone to be in charge of all the food."

What happened next must have been a big surprise for the young Hebrew. *"And Pharaoh said unto Joseph, Forasmuch as God hath shewed thee all this, there is none so discreet and wise as thou art: Thou shalt be over my house, and according unto thy word shall all my people be ruled: only in the throne will I be greater than thou"* (vs. 39-40).

Pharaoh was impressed with Joseph's God-given ability to interpret dreams. He saw that Joseph was wise and responsible, so he gave him the job. Joseph's jaw must have hit the floor! He was suddenly promoted to the second highest position in the land.

And here we see another truth concerning faith: faith is always rewarded. The Bible clearly states this in Hebrews 11:6. *"But without faith it is impossible to please him: for he that cometh to God must believe that he is, and that he is a rewarder of them that diligently seek him."*

God rewards those who seek Him by faith and place their faith in Him. Augustine said, "Faith is to believe what we do not see, and the reward of this faith is to see what we believe." Often we are doubly blessed because God answers our faith-filled request and then goes on to bless us again. We find this true with so many characters in the Bible.

Abraham put his faith in God when he had to sacrifice his son, even believing that God would raise him from the dead. God rewarded Abraham's faith. Not only could he keep his son alive, but God provided a ram to sacrifice.

Rahab put her faith in the God of Israel in order to be spared from the destruction of Jericho. God rewarded Rahab's faith. Not only was her family spared, but beyond that, God honored her by placing her in the lineage of Christ (see Matt. 1:5).

Young David put his faith in God in order to defeat the giant Goliath. God rewarded David's faith. He not only killed Goliath, but this act propelled him into the warrior he would become. God continued to reward David with victory after victory.

Solomon put his faith in God when he sincerely asked the Lord for wisdom to rule Israel. God rewarded Solomon's faith. He not only gave him incredible wisdom, but He also blessed him with great riches and fame.

Time and again, Daniel put his faith in God, living an uncompromising life of devotion and prayer. God rewarded Daniel's faith. He not only promoted him to a high position, but Daniel found favor with all the kings he served under, and was even spared when cast into the den of lions.

There at so many others (we haven't even mentioned people in the New Testament). If you want to see all the rewards which faith can obtain, read Hebrews 11:33-40, which gives a lengthy list of how faith conquered many insurmountable obstacles.

God has made it a rule to reward us for our faith. Faith is the greatest quality which we can have, and therefore God is pleased to reward us for displaying it. A dog is rewarded for obeying his master; a child is rewarded for doing his chores; an employee is rewarded for working his job diligently; and a Christian is likewise rewarded for having faith in God. But this reward far exceeds any other, for it comes from *"...the Father of lights, with whom is no variableness, neither shadow of turning"* (Jam. 1:17b).

Ultimately, our greatest reward will come in the next life, when we will receive new bodies and, if we have been faithful, crowns to cast at Jesus' feet. But God also desires to reward us in this life. I cannot say how God will reward you. It is not always with wealth and fame. But the Lord is a gracious God, and like any good father who wants to reward his children when they do right, our heavenly Father delights in blessing us for our faith.

Joseph had been through much turmoil. For years he sat in a dungeon, no doubt wondering if things would ever turn around. The moment finally came when God could surprise Joseph with an incredible reward for his faith. Christian, God loves to surprise us with blessings. Continue to live with integrity, and God will be sure to bless you for it when the time comes.

Eight
Joseph's Power

His Triumph

"And he made him to ride in the second chariot which he had; and they cried before him, Bow the knee: and he made him ruler over all the land of Egypt."
Genesis 41:43

Within one day, Joseph's life completely changed. With integrity he had served and stayed committed to God, and now God was blessing him for it. He had found favor in Pharaoh's eyes. He was no longer a slave; now he was a sovereign. When we live our lives with integrity and do right despite the consequences, no matter how long it takes, God will pour out His blessings on us for our faithfulness. The rest of Genesis chapter 41 is about the many immense blessings Joseph received.

I wonder if Potipher was in the room when this happened. He remembered Joseph as a hard-working young man. He could not believe this Hebrew slave had been promoted to such a position!

Maybe he told his wife that night, "Honey, remember Joseph, the young man you accused of molesting you?"

Her eyes grew wide. "What about him?"

"He's been promoted alongside Pharaoh. I report to him for work tomorrow morning."

My, how things had changed!

Let's examine all the blessings which Joseph received. In doing so, we can understand that such blessings are waiting for those who faithfully live for the Lord with integrity.

The Blessing of His New Position

Joseph had been appointed to the position of Grand Vizier. Bible commentator John Phillips explains: "Egyptian tombs tell us much about this office. The grand vizier was shown, for instance, receiving envoys and vice-regents from far-off lands. His chief function was to uphold the strong, centralized, authoritarian power of the throne. His tasks included keeping local princelings in check, their wings properly clipped so they might never become a threat to the pharaoh.

"He was responsible for the appointment of those inspectors charged with keeping an eye on local governors. From time to time his duties would take him to various parts of Egypt. Tomb pictures depict him receiving the homage of local officials, who are shown prostrate before him in the dust. Scribes can be seen recording his decisions. He had to probe the status of the Nile; would it be a good Nile or a bad, that is, would there be a plentiful inundation or a meager one? How were the dikes and canals? how much forced labor must be drafted to effect repairs? He would cross-question his subordinates regarding census lists, expected agricultural yield, the well-being of the herds."

To say that this position was a step up for Joseph would be a gross understatement. He was propelled to the second highest position in Egypt! A forgotten Hebrew slave was now Grand Vizier!

Pharaoh had great respect for Joseph. "I have set you over all the land of Egypt." He took off his ring and put it on Joseph's finger. He arrayed the young man in beautiful royal apparel. He put a gold chain around his neck. He gave him a brand new shining chariot of gold.

Joseph took his new ride for a spin. Crowds line the streets, waiting to see the new Grand Vizier.

"There he is!" one man shouted.

"Oh, he's so handsome," a young woman stated.

People begin to shout and cheer. "Bow the knee!"

Joseph had become ruler over all the land of Egypt (vs. 43).

Pharaoh looked at Joseph as if he were his own son. *"I am Pharaoh, and without thee shall no man lift up his hand or foot in all the land of Egypt"* (vs. 44). What a declaration! If only Joseph's brothers could see him now!

Pharaoh called Joseph by a new name: Zaphnath-paaneah. Not the most common name, but he was called this for its meaning. In Egyptian, the name meant "savior of the world." Pharaoh knew that within just seven years, all the world would be coming to Joseph for food—he would be the savior of the world.

But the name meant something else in Hebrew: "revealer of secrets." Indeed, this title fit Joseph well, for he was the dreamer, the interpreter of dreams, and more than anything, the revealer of Jehovah God. He was unashamed of his God. Now he had the opportunity to ride all across Egypt and declare who his God was. Jehovah God was the secret of his greatness.

This happened to Joseph when he was thirty years of age (vs. 46). It was the perfect age, for any younger and the Egyptians might have thought he was too young for the position. God knew what He was doing. *"And Joseph went out from the presence of Pharaoh, and went throughout all the land of Egypt"* (vs. 46b).

It was time to get to work. Like his father, Joseph was a hard worker. He had been a hard worker under his father; he was a hard worker when he worked for Potiphar; he was a hard worker in the prison; and now he would work just as hard as Grand Vizier.

The Blessing of His Bride

Now Joseph was given a beautiful bride. Her name was *Asenath*, daughter of Potipherah, priest of On. Her heritage suggests that she was an Egyptian priestess. Here was a woman who was not well known, yet was favored enough to become the bride of this great man.

I am sure that Joseph became the revealer of secrets to her as he boldly told her about his God. She would have held to the beliefs and practices of the Egyptians. They worshiped almost everything: the sun, cats, cows, jackals, insects, the Nile River, you name it. With compassion, Joseph would say, "Dear Asenath, Jehovah God made all of those things. He is the Creator of the heavens and the earth." Perhaps Asenath believed in the true God because she could see that He was real in the life of her husband.

The Blessing of Bountiful Crops

The seven years of prosperity blossomed with only the best crops. *"And in the seven plenteous years the earth brought forth by handfuls. And he gathered up all the food of the seven years, which were in the land of Egypt, and laid up the food in the cities: the food of the field, which was round about every city, laid he up in the same. And Joseph gathered corn as the sand of the sea, very much, until he left numbering; for it was without number"* (vs. 47-49).

God was blessing Egypt, not "just because," but for the sake of His servant Joseph. An entire nation was being blessed for the sake of one man, and for the purpose which only God could see.

The Blessing of His Children

Those years of prosperity not only yielded crops for Egypt, but they also yielded children for Joseph. Asenath gave birth to two sons. *"And Joseph called the name of the firstborn Manasseh: For God, said he, hath made me forget all my toil, and all my father's house"* (vs. 51).

The name *Manasseh* means "forgetting." Joseph had been so richly blessed, and he was thankful for the blessings of God. He realized that all the suffering had been worth it. The days of being bullied by his brothers were long gone. The day he was sold into slavery seemed so distant. Even the days in prison seemed like ages ago. All of those memories faded away under the massive blessings of God. "God has made me to forget all my pain and toil."

Joseph had another son. *"And the name of the second called he Ephraim: For God hath caused me to be fruitful in the land of my affliction"* (vs. 52). *Ephraim* means "fruitful." Joseph's life had seemed so barren, and the years in prison seemed like wasted years. Yet his life was now in full bloom. Not only was the land of Egypt fruitful, but Joseph's life was fruitful.

"The Blessing of the LORD, it maketh rich..."

In chapter 3 we talked about prospering. There is a difference between prospering and experiencing God's bountiful blessings. When Joseph was a slave, he prospered in the fact that he was favored and respected by others. But here Joseph experienced God's richest blessings for all the years of his faithfulness, integrity, and complete faith in God.

Every day we experience God's blessings. Just waking up in the morning is a blessing we do not deserve. But have you experienced bountiful blessings from the Lord for your faithfulness and integrity? If you will continue to live for Christ,

God will be faithful to pour out His blessings on your life and family.

Proverbs 10:22 tells us, *"The blessing of the LORD, it maketh rich, and he addeth no sorrow with it."* This was true of Joseph. He literally became rich with God's blessings. He received untold wealth with his new position, along with a wife and children. Now understand, I am not advocating that you will become rich and famous if you live for the Lord. God blesses different people in different ways. But God's blessings could make you just as rich with a wonderful new job or a bountiful family. John Calvin was right when he stated, "However many blessings we expect from God, His infinite liberality will always exceed all our wishes and our thoughts."

Notice in this verse that it also says, *"…and he addeth no sorrow with it."* God's blessings do not come with a downside. There are no negatives hidden within the blessing. It is all good, for it comes from a God who is all good. Trouble and sorrow may lead to the blessing, as we see with Joseph, but when the blessing comes, it is all rejoicing.

Has God blessed you yet with bountiful blessings? If not, then continue to walk in integrity. In time, God will pour out those blessings on your life. Integrity and blessings are connected. *"The just man walketh in his integrity: his children are blessed after him"* (Pro. 20:7).

Those seven years of plenteous went by quickly. Joseph hardly noticed them, his life was so rich and wonderful. The storehouses were full of countless crops. Then the dearth struck. Every nation began suffering except Egypt, because one man had an open line to God. When people needed bread, they went to Pharaoh, and Pharaoh in turn sent them to Joseph. "Go to Joseph. He is your savior."

Every spot on earth was hit with the famine. News began to spread that Egypt had food and supplies in store, and they were selling them to anyone who would be willing to buy. Out of desperation, people flocked to Joseph for food. They came to him for life itself. If they only knew who he was just seven short years before. . . but Joseph had long forgotten about that.

Nine
Joseph's Purpose
His Interrogations

"And Joseph remembered the dreams which he dreamed of them, and said unto them, Ye are spies; to see the nakedness of the land are ye come."
Genesis 42:9

The famine struck everywhere. Food was running out, families were starving, and life itself was becoming unbearable. In the land of Canaan, Jacob's family was impacted. Perhaps the sons were wondering why they had been affected. After all, they were in the promised land, they were the chosen family of Jehovah God. Yet God was going to use this famine to unfold an incredible event which He had planned long ago.

Jacob was a spiritual man, but he was also a sensible one. He said to his sons, *"Why do ye look one upon another?"* (Gen. 42:1). The brothers were trying to help each other, yet the famine had hurt them all. "My sons, I have heard that there is corn in Egypt. Go and buy some so we may live." They reluctantly agreed, knowing the journey would be hard, yet realizing they desperately needed the food.

The brothers were all now fully grown with families, yet they banded together for the sake of their old father and their loved ones. Only Benjamin stayed behind, who was most precious to his father. Benjamin was born of Rachel, and Jacob did not want anything to happen to him as happened to Joseph.

So the ten brothers left for Egypt. Down they went, past Beersheba into the wilderness of Zin. They crossed west into Shur and finally reached the borders of Egypt. No doubt they followed the Nile River to the place where the corn was stored. *"And Joseph was the governor over the land, and he it was that sold to all the people of the land: and Joseph's brethren came,* **and bowed down themselves before him with their faces to the earth"** (vs. 6, emphasis mine).

Joseph must have been taken aback to see his brothers, and to see his dreams fulfilled before his very eyes. He immediately knew it was them, but they did not recognize their brother. It had been twenty years since they had seen him, and Joseph had grown up.

Joseph spoke to them in the Egyptian language through an interpreter. He did not want them to recognize him. First he had to test them, and strike their consciences.

Why did Joseph go through the trouble of interrogating his brothers and testing them? He had one purpose in mind: to see if they had changed. Were they still the same ruthless men? Were they still filled with jealousy and anger? Joseph would prove them to find out. In the next three chapters, he laid several tests on them.

The Spy Test

Joseph's first test was simply to get some information from his brothers. I imagine he also wanted to see their reaction when he accused them. *"Whence come ye?"* the young governor demanded.

They answered, *"From the land of Canaan to buy food"* (vs. 7).

Joseph eyed them, perhaps looking at each one with a penetrating gaze. *"Ye are spies; to see the nakedness of the land ye are come"* (vs. 9).

They could not believe they were being accused of such a thing. *"Nay, my lord, but to buy food are thy servants come"* (vs. 10). Perhaps Reuben was the spokesman for the group. He had just called his little brother "lord." Indeed, Joseph was lord over his brethren.

Joseph again called them spies. He was waiting to hear them confess something. *"And they said, Thy servants are twelve brethren, the sons of one man in the land of Canaan; and, behold, the youngest is this day with our father, and one is not"* (vs. 13). There it was! The mention of one that was not, referring of course to Joseph, the man whom they stood before now.

But Joseph was not done with them yet. He tested them to prove that they were not spies. "If you are truly not spies, bring your youngest brother here. Send one of you and fetch him, otherwise I will know that you are spies." With that, he put them in prison for three days.

Joseph wanted his brothers to sit there and contemplate what they had done. He wanted them to remember poor Joseph when he was sold as a slave. This was not revenge at all, for Joseph could have killed them on the spot or at least roughed them up, but he justly handled them. He wanted their consciences to be pricked.

On the third day, Joseph told them, *"If ye be true men, let one of your brethren be bound in the house of your prison: go ye, carry corn for the famine of your houses: But bring your youngest brother unto me; so shall your words be verified, and ye shall not die. And they did so"* (vs. 19-20).

The brothers then huddled around and spoke of the crime they had committed so many years ago. They spoke in the Hebrew language, confident that the young Egyptian official could not understand them since he used an interpreter to talk to them. However, Joseph heard and understood every word. *"And they said one to another, We are verily guilty concerning our brother, in that we saw the anguish of his soul, when he besought us, and we would not hear; therefore is this distress come upon us. And*

Reuben answered them, saying, Spake I not unto you, saying, Do not sin against the child; and ye would not hear? therefore, behold, also his blood is required" (vs. 21-22). Finally, they realized that they were reaping what they had sown. Joseph's plan was working perfectly.

The Simeon Test

Hearing his brothers speak of him after so many years was difficult for Joseph. It took a lot of self-control not to reveal himself (no doubt he was joyful to see them). He ran into a back room and wept, then washed his face and returned to them. In the presence of the other men, Joseph took Simeon and bound him. It was fitting that he took the most violent and cruel brother. Simeon probably most wanted to kill Joseph those twenty years ago. But not for a second did they think this young ruler was Joseph.

With their sacks full of corn, they headed toward home, their hearts heavy. They sadly left Simeon (whereas, twenty years earlier, they hadn't cared less about watching another brother leave).

They made the trek back across the wilderness, through Shur, into Zin. Somewhere along the way, they stopped to rest for the night. As one of the brothers opened his sack to get food for his donkey, there was his money which he had given to pay for the corn (vs. 27). He told the others, *"and their heart failed them, and they were afraid, saying one to another, What is this that God hath done unto us?"* (vs. 28). It turned out that everyone's money was returned, and that money haunted them.

When they returned home, Jacob came out to greet them, and they told him everything that happened. As they spoke of the mysterious lord and his dealings with them, his requirement of meeting the youngest son, and the money which was found in their sacks, Jacob dropped his head in sorrow. *"Me have ye bereaved of my children: Joseph is not, and Simeon is not, and ye will take Benjamin away: all these things are against me"* (vs. 36).

Jacob had experienced great loss in his family. He had lost his most precious wife Rachel, his most precious son Joseph, and Simeon was being held captive. He did not want to lose Benjamin, his youngest and now most precious son.

Jacob's sons could not bring themselves to admit to their father that they had sold poor Joseph into slavery. To do so would crush their father. But they would not need to admit it, for soon enough Jacob would find out that Joseph was alive and well. Their sin would be put on display for all to see. *"Be sure your sin will find you out"* (Numbers 32:23).

The brothers knew they could not go back to Egypt for more food unless they took their brother Benjamin with them. They had no choice but to obey the Egyptian ruler.

Reuben spoke up. "Father, please. Let Benjamin come with us. We'll make sure nothing happens to him. We will guard him with our very lives. Kill my two sons if I do not bring him back safely to you! Let him come with me, and he will return to you safely, I promise." You never saw anyone plead like Reuben did that day. With great earnestness and fervency he pleaded, perhaps because his brother Simeon was captive, or perhaps because he wanted to do the right thing.

Could Jacob trust his son to protect Benjamin? "No, my son. I'm sorry. The risk is too great. Benjamin will not go with you."

Time passed, and eventually Jacob's family ran out of corn. Genesis chapter 43 does not tell us how long it was; perhaps just a few months, perhaps a year, perhaps two years. Whatever the case, they needed to make the trek back to Egypt to get more food. However, they knew they had to take Benjamin.

Judah spoke sensibly to his father. He did not beat around the bush, but put the facts out in the open. "Listen, Father, if we do not take Benjamin, we will get no food. That is what the man told us."

Jacob stared at him in disbelief. "Why did you tell the man you had a younger brother?"

Judah replied, "He asked us point-blank if we had a father and if we had another brother, so we told him we did. How could we have known that he would ask us to bring Benjamin down?"

Jacob was still hesitant, so Judah continued. "I'll be responsible for Benjamin. If anything happens to him, I'll take the blame." Here was a sensible solution. Unlike Reuben, Judah did not promise to have his sons executed if Benjamin did not return safely. That was a foolish thing to say. After all, how would you feel if you were one of Reuben's sons? But Judah, who just a few years before was a *sensual* man (Genesis 38), was now a *sensible* man. He was willing to take full responsibility for Benjamin's welfare.

Finally Jacob gave his permission but he made plenty of preparations. The Egyptian lord must be pleased in order to let them go in peace. Jacob commanded his sons to take a large gift with them, consisting of the best fruits, balm, honey, spices, myrrh, nuts, and almonds. On top of that, they took double the money they had before because Joseph had graciously given their money back to them. All of this was unnecessary—why would this Egyptian lord, who had everything he could ever desire, want a present from these men? Yet the brothers wanted to please the man, and also get Simeon back.

Jacob sent them away reluctantly, having no other choice. As the old patriarch leaned on his staff, he said, *"God Almighty give you mercy before the man, that he may send away your other brother, and Benjamin. If I be bereaved of my children, I am bereaved"* (vs. 14).

Jacob learned to accept what might happen. Had he not already lost his most precious wife and his most precious son (or so he thought)? He finally learned to hold loosely to the things of this earth, even his own family.

The Big Feast

The brothers set off, traveling once again to Egypt. When Joseph heard of their arrival, he told his steward, *"Bring these men home, and slay, and make ready; for these men shall dine with me at noon"* (vs. 16). Joseph planned to give them the royal treatment, but he had much more in mind than just that.

The steward approached the brothers. "The master would like all of you to join him at his house for dinner. Please follow me."

Surprised, the brothers entered the great lord's home. Egyptian carvings and tapestries beautifully adorned the interior of the house, with only the finest furniture setting in the proper place. No doubt there were incredible vases and Egyptian artifacts on display. A grandeur of fragrance met their senses, reminding them that this was a place of Egyptian royalty. They stood in a magnificent room, the likes of which they had never seen before.

As the brothers looked around, they wondered why they should be brought into the master's house. Thoughts of fear struck them. *"Because of the money that was returned in our sacks at the first time are we brought in; that he may seek occasion against us, and fall upon us, and take us for bondmen, and our asses"* (vs. 18). They could not fathom why this Egyptian ruler would want to show kindness to a group of Hebrews. It did not make sense, so they thought something terrible would happen.

They explained to the steward what happened to them the last time. They told him about the money in their sacks, and they didn't know who put it there. The steward just smiled. *"Peace be to you, fear not: your God, and the God of your father, hath given you treasure in your sacks: I had your money"* (vs. 23). Perhaps Joseph told him to say that.

Then he brought Simeon to them. They must have been excited to see Simeon still in one piece. No doubt they asked him what happened, and Simeon's reply was very simple. "Nothing happened. . . the ruler was very good to me." Joseph would not have treated Simeon harshly, but instead probably treated him with great kindness, something Simeon had never done for Joseph.

With all the brothers in the room, the steward took good care of them. He gave them water, washed their feet, and provided food for their animals. Such kindness shown to Hebrews was rare in Egypt, if ever done at all. When the steward left, the brothers prepared their present for the master. Then they waited.

When Joseph arrived, the brothers presented their gifts to him and bowed themselves to the floor. Without missing a beat, Joseph asked, *"Is your father well, the old man of whom ye spake? Is he yet alive?"* (vs. 27). That was what most concerned Joseph, for he was his father's too, and he desired to see him again. *"And they said, Thy servant our father is in good health, he is yet alive. And they bowed down their heads, and made obeisance"* (vs. 28). Joseph's mind must have raced back twenty years when he told his brothers, *"and, behold, your sheaves stood round about, and made obeisance to my sheaf"* (Gen. 37:7). Once again, he saw his dream fulfilled.

Then Joseph noticed Benjamin, whom he had not seen last time. *"Is this your younger brother, of whom ye spake unto me? And he said, God be gracious unto thee, my son"* (vs. 29). Joseph's heart started pounding; he so strongly desired to talk with his younger brother, his *only* brother, and here he was. Excusing himself, Joseph went into a private chamber and there wept, *"for his bowels did yearn upon his brother..."* (vs. 30). He washed his face, no doubt looking at himself in the mirror and saying to himself, "You can do this."

Joseph rejoined his brothers. "Let's eat!" The Egyptians ate at one table, the brothers ate together at a separate table, and Joseph ate by himself. You see, in this day it was an abomination for the Egyptians to eat with Hebrews. Since Joseph probably looked like an Egyptian, he wouldn't eat at the same table with his brothers, yet the Egyptian servants wouldn't eat at the same table with him.

Joseph had his brothers seated in a particular order, the order of their births. Reuben was first, then Simeon, then Levi, and all the way down to Benjamin at the end. *"...and the men marvelled one at another"* (vs. 33b). How did he get them in the correct birth order? It could not have been a coincidence! They should have put two and two together here, but in their minds Joseph was dead.

Joseph's servants brought out the food. The KJV called the servings "messes." The term *mess* actually comes from the Old French word *mes* meaning "a portion of food." It sounds like a sloppy term, but let me assure you, it was the finest food Egypt had to offer. Those brothers were privileged to eat the finest meats, fruits, nuts, and the finest wines. It was a feast for kings.

I imagine Reuben was served first, then Simeon, Levi, and so on. Last was Benjamin. Five servants carried his food as he received five times as much as the others! What a mess that was! Why would Joseph do that? He wanted to see if the brothers had changed. Years ago they envied the youngest to the point of almost killing him. He wanted to see if they would still envy the youngest. But they made no remark, nor did they eye Benjamin with contempt. They had changed.

Once again, they should have realized who this man was, considering his concern for Jacob, his obvious favoritism for Benjamin, and his knowledge of their order of birth. Who could know such things but Joseph? In a sense, the whole meal was a set-up. Yet Joseph was genuinely showing kindness to his brothers. But he was not done testing them yet—one final test remained.

The Benjamin Test

At the beginning of Genesis chapter 44, Joseph instituted the final test for his brothers. *"And he commanded the steward of his house, saying, Fill the men's sacks with food, as much as they can carry, and put every man's money in his sack's mouth. And put my cup, the silver cup, in the sack's mouth of the youngest, and his corn money. And he did according to the word that Joseph had spoken"* (vs. 1-2).

In the morning, the men got up and began traveling home. They thought all their troubles were over. Simeon was with them, Benjamin was safe, and they had a new supply of food. They must have been surprised to see the Egyptian steward coming after them with a band of soldiers.

Joseph told his steward what to do and say to his brothers, and the steward spoke roughly to them. "Why have you rewarded evil for good?"

"What are you talking about?" they replied.

"Where is my lord's divining cup? You have stolen it!"

Concerning the divining cup, John Phillips informs us: "In ancient Egypt a goblet was frequently used as a means of communicating with the spirits. In some cases small pieces of gold or silver, together with precious stones, were cast into the goblet over which appropriate incantations were uttered. The cup then acted as a species of Ouija board. Sometimes the goblet would be filled with water and set in the sun so that the deeps and shadows cast in the cup could be read just as some people today read tea leaves in a cup." I highly doubt Joseph used this cup in such a manner since he was a believer in Jehovah God, but he was playing a part in this test for his brothers.

The men were confident they had not stolen the cup, perhaps a little too confident. *"With whomsoever of thy servants it be found, both let him die, and we also will be my lord's bondmen"* (vs. 9). The steward must have grinned. He knew exactly what would happen, for he too was playing a part in Joseph's game.

He started with the oldest and then moved all the way down to the youngest. The cup was found in Benjamin's sack. Here was the test which Joseph had set forth. Would the brothers let Benjamin go and leave him in Egypt as they had done to Joseph? Or would they do everything in their power to plead for him and bring him back with them? Had their hearts changed since their last diabolical plot, or were they still the same?

Benjamin was Jacob's most precious son. *"If mischief befall him by the way in the which ye go, then shall ye bring down my gray hairs with sorrow to the grave"* (Gen. 42:38b). With those words ringing in their ears, the brothers rent their clothes and made the short journey back to Egypt. If Benjamin stayed in Egypt or was executed, it would crush Jacob, no doubt putting him in an early grave. They could not let that happen.

They were thrust before a furious Joseph who would now show them his full power and authority. *"What deed is this that ye have done? wot ye not that such a man as I can certainly divine?"* (vs. 15).

Judah stepped forward and became the spokesman for the eleven. "What shall we say, my lord? God has discovered our iniquity! We are your servants." But Joseph put the pressure on the sore spot, so to speak. He wanted to see their reaction. *"God forbid that I should do so: but the man in whose hand the cup is found, he shall be my servant: and as for you, get you up in peace unto your father"* (vs. 17).

Judah proved, beyond a doubt, that he had a change of heart. *"Then Judah came near unto him, and said, Oh my lord, let thy servant, I pray thee, speak a word in my lord's ears, and let not thine anger burn against thy servant: **for thou art even as Pharaoh**"* (vs. 18, emphasis mine).

Judah recognized Joseph's position. Their lives were in his hand, and he could do to them whatever he wanted. Truly, the sheaves were bowing, recognizing and submitting to the powerful ruler who stood before them.

Judah continued, speaking about his father. *"And we said unto my lord, We have a father, an old man, and a child of his old age, a little one; **and his brother is dead**, and he alone is left of his mother, and his father loveth him"* (vs. 20, emphasis mine).

Notice what he said concerning Joseph. They all thought Joseph was dead, and no doubt they felt responsible for his death. Or perhaps, because they had convinced their father Joseph was dead, they convinced themselves too. Judah explained Jacob's love and affection for Benjamin, and how reluctant he was to let Benjamin go. But in the end, he let him go with them. "You see, my lord, if our father sees that the lad is not with us when we return, he will die, and I will bear the blame because I promised his safety."

Now we see the real change in Judah as he made an amazing intercessory prayer. *"Now therefore, I pray thee, let thy servant abide instead of the lad a bondman to my lord; and let the lad go up with his brethren. For how shall I go up to my father, and the lad be not with me? lest peradventure I see the evil that shall come on my father"* (vs. 33-34).

Judah was willing to substitute himself for Benjamin. "Take me as your servant instead, and let the lad go." What a sacrifice he is willing to make! This does not sound like the Judah of chapter 37 who suggested that they sell Joseph to the Ishmeelites and make a profit. Now he is submissive and sacrificial. What a change! No wonder God chose to use this man and his line to bring the Messiah into the world. For in this instance, Judah is a perfect picture of the Savior, willing to substitute himself that Benjamin may go free, and that his father may live.

Joseph must have been very pleased to see this man, once cruel and cunning, now careful and caring. His brothers had passed the tests; they had had a change of heart. Their conscience and their Creator had been hammering away at them, and they had been chiseled down to men of character.

We Need Testing

Joseph tested his brothers and discovered that they had changed for the better. In the same way, God often tests us to see if we have changed. He wants to see if we trust Him and love Him, or if we're nothing but phonies.

Job was greatly tested by God. At first, Job did not curse God. But over time, as the weeks passed, Job became bitter against God. We see the climax of this bitterness in Job 16:9, where Job said about his Creator, *"He teareth me in his wrath, who hateth me: he gnasheth upon me with his teeth; mine enemy sharpeneth his eyes upon me."*

In this verse, Job thought God hated him. He called the Lord his enemy. By the end of the book, we find that Job failed the test as God asked him question after question that he could not answer. Yet we know Job understood something about the tests God gave him. He made an amazing statement in Job 23:10: *"But he knoweth the way that I take: when he hath tried me, I shall come forth as gold."*

Gold is often given the "acid test" to determine its value. Because gold is resistant to change by corrosion, oxidation, or acid, it is easy to test it simply by applying a drop of nitric acid. The finer the gold, the less the acid will affect it. But if it has impurities, such as other metals mixed in, the acid will oxidize and leave a coppery brown spot. It is not pure gold.

Many times in life God will let you go through problems, fears, and difficult obstacles. During these times, He's testing you to see if you have the integrity to pull through. If not, then you need more time in the fire. But if you have golden character, you'll pass God's acid test.

Joseph experienced some big tests and he passed them all. He came out as pure gold. Then he was able to test his brothers, and they passed as well. God gives great blessings to those who pass the test. Just look at Joseph's brothers. In the next chapter they all moved into Egypt, where Joseph was able to bless them and take care of them. No more problems. No more worries.

Men with golden character are the men who will receive the golden blessings.

Many times in the Lord's will let you go through problem, fear, and difficult obstacles. During those times He's testing you to see if you have the strength to pull through it. For you who is struggling in life, rec that you have gotten this far, still here today, and you

[illegible faded text continues — not clearly readable]

Ten
Joseph's Promise
His Forgiveness

"But as for you, ye thought evil against me; but God meant it unto good, to bring to pass, as it is this day, to save much people alive."
Genesis 50:20

The time had come. Joseph could not stand it any longer, he had to tell his brothers the truth. *"Cause every man to go out from me"* (Gen. 45:1). Joseph was now alone with his brothers. He began to weep very loudly, so loud that *"the Egyptians and the house of Pharaoh heard"* (vs. 2). No man ever wept like that before. It was an amazing weeping of joy, of relief, of reunion—he was weeping over his brethren. Joseph's brothers no doubt looked around at each other, feeling awkward.

"And Joseph said unto his brethren, I am Joseph; doth my father yet live? And his brethren could not answer him; for they were troubled at his presence" (vs. 3). They did not shout for joy; instead they were paralyzed with fear. They didn't believe him the first time. It couldn't be true.

Joseph brought them closer to him. "I am Joseph, whom you sold into Egypt, remember? I'm not going to harm you. God has sent me here to preserve life." He recognized that their evil plot to sell him turned into God's eternal plan to use him as the savior of the world.

Joseph also mentioned that there would be five more years of the terrible famine. *"And God sent me before you to preserve you a posterity in the earth, and to save your lives by a great deliverance. So now it was not you that sent me hither, but God: and he hath made me a father to Pharaoh, and lord of all his house, and a ruler throughout all the land of Egypt"* (vs. 7-8). Joseph had not been put through the fires of God's testing for nothing; he recognized that all this happened because of God. "My brothers, God sent me here."

If he had known the verse, he would have quoted it: *"And we know that all things work together for good to them that love God, to them who are the called according to his purpose"* (Rom. 8:28). Joseph knew about that before it was ever penned. He knew that God Almighty could turn a tragedy into a triumph. He knew that a sovereign God was in control of all the situations he had been through. He knew that God had graciously preserved him and used him not just to help others, but to save his own family.

Joseph had a plan. His plan first involved **the father**. *"Haste ye, and go up to my father, and say unto him, Thus saith thy son Joseph, God hath made me lord of all Egypt: come down unto me, tarry not"* (vs. 9). How thrilled the father would be to hear that his son whom was dead now lived! It was as if he had risen from the dead.

Joseph's plan also involved **a big move**. *"And thou shalt dwell in the land of Goshen, and thou shalt be near unto me, thou, and thy children, and thy children's children, and thy flocks, and thy herds, and all that thou hast"* (vs. 10). Joseph wanted the best for his family. They needed to move where blessing and prosperity dwelt. "Come and live with me; I have many mansions."

Joseph's plan also involved **provision and prosperity.** *"And there will I nourish thee; for yet there are five years of famine; lest thou, and thy household, and all that thou hast, come to poverty"* (vs. 11). Joseph made a great promise to provide for his own family. "I will supply all your needs through the riches of my grace." He had become the Great Provider, only because God had blessed him so. Joseph added a personal note. *"And, behold, your eyes see, and the eyes of my brother Benjamin, that it is my mouth that speaketh unto you"* (vs. 12). It had finally sunk in—this man was Joseph! He looked different, yet not they recognized him. Everything he had said was true. His promises could be trusted.

Finally, Joseph's plan involved **his glory.** *"And ye shall tell my father of all my glory in Egypt, and of all that ye have seen; and ye shall haste and bring down my father hither"* (vs. 13). Until now, Joseph's glory had been veiled, but now the brothers could see his glory. With excitement, they could say, "We beheld his glory." With great joy they were to tell their father of Joseph and his glory.

No doubt you have seen the parallels, for they are magnificent. Jesus Christ is clearly seen in every instance, and it takes our breath away.

The Father

Joseph gave his brothers provision for their journey, making sure they had everything they needed. But to Benjamin he gave far more: he gave him three hundred pieces of silver, and five changes of raiment. He wanted to see again if the others would be envious in any way, but they did not even notice. They were all blessed so much. With great joy they set off for home with nothing but *good news* to tell! They had come to Egypt with nothing, seeking corn, but they were going home with everything, seeking to tell their father the news.

Joseph gave them a great present for their father: ten donkeys covered in good things of Egypt, and ten female donkeys carrying corn, bread, and meat. He sent them away with a final word of warning. *"See that ye fall not out by the way"* (vs. 24b). He set them on the straight and narrow path.

When they arrived home, Jacob must have been shocked to see all those donkeys carrying stuff from Egypt!

Jacob looked at them. "What's going on?"

"All of this is for you, Father." Judah must have been the one to break the news. "Your son Joseph is alive!"

"And Jacob's heart fainted, for he believed them not" (vs. 26). Joseph couldn't be alive, old Jacob thought. He had received his coat all torn to pieces and covered in blood. But then the confession issues forth, the deceitful act which so many years ago had taken place. The brothers were now forced to confess what they had done. Jacob couldn't believe it. But then they began to tell their old father of Joseph and his glory.

Jacob must have smiled, then laughed. He had not experienced such sheer joy since his meeting with God at Bethel. His son was alive! Prosperity was awaiting him in Egypt! The blessings of God had never been greater. His family was reunited, his faith was rekindled, and his focus was readjusted. It was like Jacob was made a new man. He believed this wonderful gospel, and his spirit was revived. *"And Israel said, It is enough; Joseph my son is yet alive: I will go and see him before I die"* (vs. 28).

The Big Move

As Genesis 46 opens, Jacob and all his sons and their families set off for the land of Egypt. When they reached Beersheba, Jacob stopped to sacrifice to God. No doubt he was concerned about this move. His grandfather Abraham had lied about his wife in Egypt (Gen. 12:10-20) with awful consequences, and his father Isaac had been forbidden to go there (Gen. 26:2). Jacob wondered if this was the right thing to do.

God confirmed it. *"And God spake unto Israel in the visions of the night, and said, Jacob, Jacob. And he said, Here am I. And he said, I am God, the God of thy father: fear not to go down into Egypt; for I will there make of thee a great nation: I will go down with thee into Egypt; and I will also surely bring thee up again: and Joseph shall put his hand upon thine eyes"* (vs. 2-4).

So with all their people, possessions, and profit, the children of Israel reached Egypt. Jacob sent Judah ahead to Joseph to prepare them to enter Goshen. Judah was now a godly man. He had interceded on behalf of Benjamin, and God would greatly bless him.

After twenty-two years, Joseph finally saw his father again. This time, Joseph did not wear a coat of many colors, but a regal robe. They must have stared at each other for just a moment, then embraced and wept for "a good while" (vs. 29). The father and the son were reunited. It was a time of great joy. *"...for this thy brother was dead, and is alive again; and was lost, and is found"* (Luke 15:32b). The brothers looked on, and no doubt wept themselves. They had put their father through much grief, yet incredible joy came out of it all. *"And Israel said unto Joseph, Now let me die, since I have seen thy face, because thou art yet alive"* (vs. 30).

Provision and Prosperity

Joseph became a mediator for his family as he went before Pharaoh on their behalf. Jacob and his family would not have been able to get into Goshen without Joseph interceding for them, and Joseph would not have been able to intercede for them if he was not in such a high position, second only to Pharaoh.

Joseph explained to his brothers what to say. By telling Pharaoh they were shepherds, they would be placed on the outskirts of Egypt in the land of Goshen. Shepherds were abominable to Egyptians, and they did not want them to be living among them. But Joseph did not want his family living among the Egyptians. He knew what was best for them.

After presenting five brothers and his old father to Pharaoh, Joseph placed his family in the land of Goshen and gave them the best of the land. Only the best! Moses called it the land of Rameses. Joseph nourished his family with bread. He provided for their needs.

Joseph's Glory

The years of famine continued, and people kept coming to buy food. Eventually, families ran out of money. They asked Joseph for help, and he advised them to sell him their cattle and their land in return for corn and wheat. As a result, Joseph bought all the land of Egypt, and the land became Pharaoh's. Once again, his foresight prevented a disaster.

Joseph started placing people in certain areas of the land, filling up the land of Egypt so that it was evenly populated. What a man he was! Joseph might have been the greatest businessman, the greatest politician, the greatest provider, the greatest trader, the greatest financier, and the greatest real estate agent in history! Not just Egypt, but the whole world was coming to him.

Perhaps it was on a sunny day when Joseph stood by the Nile River and gave a speech to thousands of people standing and applauding him as an incredible leader. Joseph had a great plan, and he was about to reveal it to the masses. *"Then Joseph said unto the people, Behold, I have bought you this day and your land for Pharaoh: lo, here is seed for you, and ye shall sow the land. And it shall come to pass in the increase, that ye shall give the fifth part unto Pharaoh, and four parts shall be your own, for seed of the field, and for your food, and for them of your households, and for food for your little ones"* (Gen. 47:23-24).

Joseph, with God's blessing and insight, had saved these people. They clapped and cheered. Some even shouted out, *"Thou hast saved our lives!"* (vs. 25). Joseph had become the savior of the world.

Did he ever dream that he would have the attention of the whole world? Did he know that one day he would stand before countless multitudes of people? Did he know that his life's story would be placed into the canon of Scripture, and that millions of people would read of his sufferings and his glory, and be moved by the Spirit of God? Christian, do not underestimate your life, or what God can do with it.

The Power of Forgiveness

As we finally reach Genesis 50, Jacob died. The old patriarch had lived a full life and had seen amazing things. Joseph, along with a huge company, went to Canaan in order to bury his father in his desired place: the cave of Machpelah, where Abraham and Sarah were buried. This was his final wish and he got it.

When they returned into Egypt, Joseph's brethren were afraid that Joseph would now enact his revenge on them. To think like this was almost to mock Joseph, for he had forgiven them long ago. Yet, out of fear and guilt, they sent a messenger to him. *"Thy father did command before he died, saying, So shall ye say unto Joseph, Forgive, I pray thee now, the trespass of thy brethren, and their sin; for they did thee evil: and now, we pray thee, forgive the trespass of the servants of the God of thy father"* (vs. 16-17).

I find it ridiculous that Jacob had to tell them to say this. These were fully grown men, capable of making their own choices and responsible for their own actions, and yet Jacob had to tell them, "Now listen, my sons, be sure to ask Joseph to forgive you for your trespass against him." And here they are: "Father told us to make sure you forgive us..." They feared Joseph, but they inserted the name of their father, thinking it would help.

However, the entire request was unnecessary. When Joseph heard these words, he wept. *"And Joseph said unto them, Fear not: for am I in the place of God?"* (vs. 19). Joseph recognized his place, and he had no desire for revenge in his heart. He truly loved his brethren, despite what they had done to him. Joseph then made an incredible statement, and it is here that we see the real power of forgiveness.

"But as for you, ye thought evil against me; but God meant it unto good, to bring to pass, as it is this day, to save much people alive" (vs. 20). What an amazing verse! Let's look at three life-changing truths concerning forgiveness in this verse.

Forgiveness recognizes the wrong

Right away, Joseph admitted, *"Ye thought evil against me."* A forgiving person will not gloss over the wrong that's been done to him, but will recognize it. We tend to hold onto the hurt we've experienced. To forgive someone of that wrong does not mean that we ignore the hurt or act like it never happened. To do this would be to live in denial.

When someone hurts you, the best thing to do is to confront them and let them know that they hurt you, even if it was something small that simply hurt your feelings. This is the first step of forgiveness.

To not take this first step is dangerous. If someone has hurt you and you are not willing to tell them, that hurt could build up inside you to the point of bitterness or revenge. How sad that many families have been torn apart by bitterness. You need to confront the person who hurt you.

If we are not willing to recognize the wrong, many times we cannot move on with our lives. Jesus taught in Matthew 5:23-24, *"Therefore if thou bring thy gift to the altar, and there rememberest that thy brother hath ought against thee; Leave there thy gift before the altar, and go thy way; first be reconciled to thy brother, and then come and offer thy gift."*

If someone has hurt you, recognize it and talk to them. Take care of it first before it becomes a big problem. Don't gloss over it or deny it, deal with it.

Perhaps you're wondering about Joseph. For many years he was separated from his brothers, and therefore he could not confront them. But he recognized it on his own and chose to forgive them. They knew what they had done was wrong, and they were haunted by it. Joseph had conquered it many years prior.

Forgiveness recognizes the sovereignty of God

After you've recognized the wrong, you need to recognize the Lord's role in the situation.

Joseph said, *"...but God meant it unto good."* God was involved in the story. He allowed it all to happen. How quickly we can blame the Lord for our problems and difficult circumstances, but God wants to use them to bring triumph out of tragedy.

"What good can come out of this divorce?"

"What good can come of my rebellious son or daughter?"

"What good can come of this relationship?"

How cynical we are. Give it to the Lord, then wait and see. I can guarantee that God is working to produce something beautiful in your life. Romans 8:28 assures us, *"And we know that all things work together for good to them that love God, to them who are the called according to his purpose."*

When you are in the midst of a trial, that is the time when you must recognize the sovereignty of God. Sitting in the dungeon, Joseph must have learned to accept the circumstances and recognize that God was in control. Don't forget God in those trying times!

The connection between forgiveness and recognizing God's sovereignty can be difficult. Who has wronged you? Realize that God has allowed that person to wrong you. We impulsively think, "Why would God let that happen?" This kind of thinking is selfish. God has the whole picture in mind. He wants to make something wonderful out of your life, and He may need to use painful means to do it. A butterfly can soar only after it has been trapped in a cocoon, then forced to fight and wiggle its way out to freedom. A certain amount of time is required before it can come out as a beautiful creature.

God works the same way. Don't ever think that God wants to hurt you by putting you in difficult circumstances. The end result will be worth it all. Today God looks at you and says, *"For I know the thoughts that I think toward you, saith the LORD, thoughts of peace, and not of evil, to give you an expected end"* (Jer. 29:11).

Forgiveness changes lives

After recognizing the wrong and the sovereignty of God, Joseph said, *"...to bring to pass, as it is this day, to save much people alive."*

This could only happen because Joseph chose to forgive his brothers.

Imagine if Joseph had become bitter against them. That bitterness would have ruined his leadership, consuming his heart with hatred. As soon as the brothers showed up, he would have executed them on the spot. His entire demeanor would have been tainted with hatred. People would come to him for food, and his generosity would be slim, if existent at all. Perhaps some would be turned away and starve.

The choice to forgive can impact many lives. But the opposite is also true: the choice to *not* forgive can negatively impact others. Once again, families have been destroyed by bitterness, but other families have been restored through forgiveness. Joseph's family is an example of that.

As Christians, we have every right to forgive those who hurt us, no matter how severe it may be. Ephesians 4:32 proclaims, *"And be ye kind one to another, tenderhearted, forgiving one another, even as God for Christ's sake hath forgiven you."* If Christ can forgive us of all our sin, we should certainly forgive anyone of any kind of wrong they have committed against us.

Jesus took it a step further when He said, *"For if ye forgive men their trespasses, your heavenly Father will also forgive you: But if ye forgive not men their trespasses, neither will your Father forgive your trespasses"* (Matt. 6:14-15). We have no right to have God's forgiveness if we do not forgive others. Forgiveness is not always an easy choice, but it is always the right choice. And by forgiving that person, his life might be changed for the better.

A man of integrity is a man of forgiveness. He does not hold grudges or become bitter. He chooses to do the right thing, no matter how hard it may be. It takes real integrity to forgive, and this is exactly what Joseph chose to do.

Conclusion

He faced persecution and problems, but with patience and perseverance, Joseph's life ended in faith. Through and through, he was a man of untouchable integrity. He displayed his character to his family, his co-workers, his authorities, and even to his enemies. He openly and boldly spoke of his God, knowing that He was sovereign and in control of all things. Joseph was an able leader, a man with compassion and purpose.

But before we close this deep look at his life, there are a couple other facets we must notice at the end of Joseph's life. One has to do with his father's blessing on him and his seed. The other has to do with Joseph's death, and the incredible faith he had during his last days.

Joseph, a Fruitful Bough

In Genesis 49, Jacob prophetically described

the futures of his sons' tribes. The depictions he gave accurately described the men's characters. Notice what old Jacob had to say about Joseph:

Joseph is a fruitful bough, even a fruitful bough by a well; whose branches run over the wall: The archers have sorely grieved him, and shot at him, and hated him: But his bow abode in strength, and the arms of his hands were made strong by the hands of the mighty God of Jacob; (from thence is the shepherd, the stone of Israel:) Even by the God of thy father, who shall help thee; and by the Almighty, who shall bless thee with blessings of heaven above, blessings of the deep that lieth under, blessings of the breasts, and of the womb: The blessings of thy father have prevailed above the blessings of my progenitors unto the utmost bound of the everlasting hills: they shall be on the head of Joseph, and on the crown of the head of him that was separate from his brethren.

Genesis 49:22-26

More than anything, Joseph could be described as a fruitful bough. His vine had grown, his branches had extended, more grapes had blossomed; truly, Joseph was far more blessed than any of his brethren. No doubt verses 23 and 24 are describing what Joseph went through with his brothers—they shot at him and wounded him, yet his hands were made strong by Almighty God.

The phrase "the shepherd, the stone of Israel" referred to the Messiah, but notice it said "from thence," meaning he came out of a different tribe, not from the tribe of Joseph. Joseph's tribe was characterized by fruitfulness, which was fulfilled in his double tribe, Ephraim and Manasseh. Because of this, Joseph was given two portions of the land (Ezek. 47:13). He was more fruitful than his brothers. Joshua, the mighty leader who took charge of Israel after Moses, was from the tribe of Ephraim (see Num. 13:8-- "Oshea" is Joshua).

Christian, consider what you will leave behind. If, like Joseph, you will be a man of integrity, you too can be a fruitful bough, and God will greatly bless your children and grandchildren. Despite the persecution and problems, keep your integrity, and don't lose your faith in God. In a world of many barren boughs, you can be fruitful, blessed by Almighty God.

The Faith of a Dying Man

Moses chose to end the book of Genesis with the death of Joseph. However, Moses did not record this just for the sake of it; Joseph's death was very significant.

Joseph was 110 years old and ready to die. He was blessed to see Ephraim's children of the third generation, and Manasseh's grandchildren too. Can you see Joseph as a grandfather, holding those children on his knees, recalling the great stories of Genesis? They listened with rapt attention as he told the story of Noah and the flood, the suspenseful tale of Isaac being sacrificed, the exciting adventures of Jacob. Then he faithfully relates God's grace and mercy to himself.

Joseph knew he was going to die, so he gathered his brethren around to tell them something very important. *"And Joseph said unto his brethren, I die: and God will surely visit you, and bring you out of this land unto the land which he sware to Abraham, to Isaac, and to Jacob"* (Gen. 50:24).

Joseph was dwelling in the land of Egypt, but he clung to the promises of God, knowing that one day God would bring the Israelites out of Egypt and back into the land of Canaan. *"And Joseph took an oath of the children of Israel, saying, God will surely visit you, and ye shall carry up my bones from hence"* (vs. 25).

The bones of Joseph were almost sacred to the children of Israel. They were the promise of the final patriarch that God would one day fulfill His promise to Abraham. It was a guarantee. "You will carry my bones out of Egypt." Four hundred years later, when Moses led the charge out of Egypt, the Bible tells us, *"And Moses took the bones of Joseph with him: for he had straitly sworn the children of Israel, saying, God will surely visit you; and ye shall carry my bones away hence with you"* (Ex. 13:19). So when the Israelites left Egypt, Joseph left with them. For years he lived in and ruled Egypt, but he certainly did not belong there.

Joseph did not want an Egyptian tomb built for him. He did not care for all of that ritualistic nonsense. He was just a sojourner in the land of Egypt—his real home was in heaven. He would rather have his bones in a box than have his body in a building. With the final words given from the final patriarch, Joseph died. Notice the last verse of Genesis: *"So Joseph died, being a hundred and ten years old: and they embalmed him, and he was put in a coffin in Egypt"* (vs. 26).

Thus Joseph died in faith, further substantiated by the words in Hebrews 11:22, *"By faith Joseph, when he died, made mention of the departing of the children of Israel; and gave commandment concerning his bones."* Joseph believed God's promise to Abraham that the Israelites would become a great nation and dwell in the land of Canaan. He died believing that. He was a man of integrity to the very end.

It is glorious when a Christian can die with integrity. At the end of his life, the Apostle Paul could say, *"I have fought a good fight, I have finished my course, I have kept the faith"* (II Tim. 4:7). He died with integrity.

At the end of your life, you will say one of two things: either "I wish I had…" or "I'm glad I did." To end your life with no regrets is quite remarkable, but it's certainly possible. The answer is to live with integrity, as Joseph did.

Will You be like Joseph?

Let's review the characteristics of Joseph's life which we have seen in this book:

1. **Joseph was a dreamer.** If you're going to do anything for God, you need to dream big, and don't let go of those dreams.
2. **Joseph was persecuted for his dreams.** You may face opposition and rejection, but remember that God will never forsake you (Heb. 13:5).
3. **Joseph prospered because of his character.** When you're living for the Lord, despite your circumstances, you will prosper and be blessed.
4. **Joseph was falsely accused despite his integrity.** God will often test your character to see if you will come out as gold.
5. **Joseph showed compassion to those who needed it.** Even during difficult times, don't focus on yourself; reach out and show compassion to others.
6. **Joseph was patient in waiting for God's timing.** God often makes us wait for the things we want the most, so learn to wait for God's timetable.

7. **Joseph showed great faith in God when interpreting Pharaoh's dream.** God will prepare you for the make-or-break moment, and faith will be needed during that time.
8. **Joseph experienced a huge turnaround as he became Grand Vizier.** God can flip the tables around in your life and bless you immeasurably if you will show integrity through the tough times.
9. **Joseph tested his brothers to see if they had changed.** After you have come out of the tough times, God may test you to see if you have really changed for the better.
10. **Joseph lovingly forgave his brothers for their wrongs against him.** No matter who is to blame for the problems you faced, learn to forgive others as Christ has forgiven you (Eph. 4:32).

Joseph's life is a challenge to us. Can we really be like this man of God? Don't forget that Joseph was not a super Christian; he was just a regular man who chose to live with integrity and be committed to God. You can choose to do the same thing.

We live in a world of wickedness. There are not many Josephs out there. Social media has influenced us to be selfish and narcissistic. We have no dreams; we're just trying to "get by." We let the tough times beat us up instead of turning to the One who can give us strength. We aren't willing to wait during those years in the dungeon.

We need to stop focusing on self and start focusing on the Savior. Remember, God has a plan, and He wants to work all things out for your good. But you must be the one to have the integrity to keep going forward.

Let me remind you of God's sovereignty in your life. Romans 8:28 says, *"And we know that all things work together for good to them that love God, to them who are the called according to his purpose."* God can take the difficult circumstances in your life and work them out for your good, if you will let Him.

Also, don't forget the great promise of Jeremiah 29:11, *"For I know the thoughts that I think toward you, saith the LORD, thoughts of peace, and not of evil, to give you an expected end."* God will never do anything to hurt you, only to help you. He has an expected end in mind for your life, and it is glorious. But if you want to reach that end, you will have to live with integrity. In today's culture, it is the only way to live.

Jesus never promised it would be easy, but He did promise that He would always be with you. *"...and lo, I am with you alway, even unto the end of the world. Amen"* (Matt. 28:20b).

So dream big, push on, and put your faith in God for those trying times, and you will come out as gold on the other side.

Joseph, a Perfect Type of Christ

Types of Christ in the Bible are fascinating, and they're all over the place. Isaac's birth pictured the birth of Christ; his sacrifice on Mount Moriah pictured the death of Christ. Melchizedek pictured Christ as Priest, Moses as Prophet, and David as King. Christ can even be seen in the feasts and offerings. But no one in the Bible pictures Christ more perfectly than Joseph. Almost every facet of his life is a parallel to Christ in some way! Perhaps you've already seen many of them as we've gone through this story.

This study is so fascinating I had to include it in this book. Leaving it out would be a missed opportunity. As we look at these, realize that only the Living God could put something so amazing together. These are not coincidences, but rather fingerprints of Jehovah God at work.

1. Joseph was the firstborn son of Rachel, and was beloved of his father (Gen. 37:3). Jesus Christ was also the firstborn (Rom. 8:29; Col. 1:15, 18; Heb. 12:23), and was also beloved of the Father (John 15:9; 17:23, 26).
2. Joseph's name means "adding." The first Adam took something away from us: righteousness. The last Adam added it to us again. *"As it is written, He hath dispersed abroad; he hath given to the poor: his righteousness remaineth for ever. Now he that ministereth seed to the sower both minister bread for your food, and multiply your seed sown, **and increase the fruits of your righteousness**"* (II Cor. 9:9-10, emphasis mine).
3. Joseph was a shepherd (Gen. 37:2); Christ is the Good Shepherd Who cares for the sheep and knows each one by name (John 10:11).
4. Joseph was against the wickedness of his brothers. *"...and Joseph brought unto his father their evil report"* (Gen. 37:2b).

Christ testified against the wickedness of the world. *"The world cannot hate you; but me it hateth, because I testify of it,* ***that the works thereof are evil****"* (John 7:7, emphasis mine).

5. Joseph was despised of his own brethren (Gen. 37:4); Christ was also despised. *"He is despised and rejected of men. . . he was despised, and we esteemed him not"* (Isa. 53:3). Christ was even despised by his own brethren. *"He came unto his own, and his own received him not"* (John 1:11).

6. Joseph was hated for his dreams, which he told publicly (Gen. 37:5); Christ was hated for His teachings, which He taught publicly. Joseph's dreams made him superior to his brethren; Christ's teachings made Him equal with God (John 10:32-33).

7. Joseph was arrayed in a coat of many colors, a gift from his father (Gen. 37:3); Christ was arrayed in glory, the glory of the Father (John 1:14).

8. Joseph's dream of the sheaves in the field

(Gen. 37:7) pictured Christ's work on earth; his dream of the sun, moon, and stars (Gen. 37:9) pictured Christ's glory in heaven. Thus Christ was worshiped on earth, and He will certainly be worshiped in heaven.

9. Joseph was sent of his father to seek his brothers; he even said, *"I seek my brethren"* (Gen. 37:16). Christ came seeking His brethren as well, the lost sheep of the house of Israel (Matt. 10:6, 15:24). *"For the Son of man is come to seek and to save that which was lost"* (Luke 19:10).

10. Joseph's brothers plotted to kill him (Gen. 37:18); in the same way, the Jews plotted how they could kill Jesus (Mark 14:1; Luke 22:2).

11. Joseph was stripped of his coat of many colors and cast in a pit (Gen. 37:23-24); Christ was stripped of his robe and placed on a cross (Matt. 27:28). It could be said of both, *"...yet we did esteem him stricken, smitten of God, and afflicted"* (Isa. 53:4b).

12. Joseph was sold as a slave for twenty

pieces of silver (Gen. 37:28); Christ was betrayed and sold for thirty pieces of silver, the price of a slave at that time (Matt. 26:15). Notice that *Judah* was the one who decided to sell Joseph, and it was *Judas* who sold our Savior.

13. Joseph being cast into a pit pictures Christ being placed in a tomb; Joseph was brought out of the pit alive, and Christ came out of the tomb alive. This is not the most perfect parallel, for we do not know how long Joseph was in the pit (certainly not for three days). Jonah is the best type of Christ in the tomb. As Jonah was in the whale's belly for three days and nights, so Christ was in the heart of the earth for three days and nights (Matt. 12:40).

14. Joseph's brothers presented his coat, covered in blood, to their father (Gen. 37:32); Jesus Christ presented His blood to the Father after His resurrection (Heb. 9:14; see also John 20:17).

15. Joseph had favor with those around him in Egypt (Gen. 39:2-4); Christ Himself "...

increased in wisdom and stature, and in favour with God and man" (Luke 2:52).

16. Joseph became a servant. *"And Joseph found grace in his sight, and he served him..."* (Gen. 39:4a). Christ was also a servant. *"For even the Son of man came not to be ministered unto, but to minister, and to give his life a ransom for many"* (Mark 10:45).

17. Joseph's master was well pleased with him (Gen. 39:4); the Father was very pleased with Jesus Christ. Jesus could honestly say, *"I do always those things that please him"* (John 8:29).

18. Joseph was tempted several times, yet sinned not (Gen. 39:7-10); Christ was tempted many times by Satan, yet He never sinned (Matt. 4:1-10).

19. Joseph used good reasoning when he was tempted (Gen. 39:8-9); Christ used Scripture to fight off the devil (Matt. 4:4, 7, 10).

20. Joseph appealed to God: *"How then can I do this great wickedness, and sin against*

God?" (Gen. 39:9b). Christ also appealed to God: *"It is written again, Thou shalt not tempt the Lord thy God"* (Matt. 4:7). In this area of temptation both were very strong. There is no one in the Bible who compares with Joseph when it comes to temptation, except, of course, Christ, Who never sinned.

21. Joseph was falsely accused (Gen. 39:14-18); likewise Christ was falsely accused. *"Now the chief priests, and elders, and all the council, sought false witness against Jesus, to put him to death; But found none: yea, though many false witnesses came, yet found they none"* (Matt. 26:59-60). Then two false witnesses came and accused Jesus of blasphemy. For this, Jesus was put to death; Joseph was cast into prison.

22. Joseph did not defend himself, but kept silent; likewise Christ opened not His mouth, but as a lamb to the slaughter, He kept silent (Isa. 53:7). Christ. . . *"did no sin, neither was guile found in his mouth:*

Who, when he was reviled, reviled not again; when he suffered, he threatened not; but committed himself to him that judgeth righteously" (I Pet. 2:22-23).

23. Joseph was cast into prison as the result of these false accusations. It is apparent that Potiphar did not believe his wife, for if he did, he would have killed the Hebrew. Instead he cast him into prison to appease his wife. Likewise, Pilate did not believe Christ to be guilty (Matt. 27:24), but sentenced Him to death simply to appease the crowd.

24. Joseph was numbered with the transgressors; he was placed in prison with two others, the butler and the baker (Gen. 40:1-3). Christ was hanged along with two malefactors (Luke 23:32). The analogy here is quite remarkable. Joseph predicted that one would be restored and the other hanged; it happened just as he said. One of the malefactors believed on Christ, and He promised him paradise; the other was condemned because of his

unbelief.

25. Joseph desired to be remembered (Gen. 40:14). Likewise Christ stated these words at the Last Supper: *"This do in remembrance of me"* (Luke 22:19).

26. Joseph waited in prison in obscurity for many years; likewise the first thirty years of Christ's life have often been called "the years of obscurity." No one knew Who He was or what He would soon do.

27. Joseph was taken out of prison and exalted on high; Pharaoh said to him, *"Thou shalt be over my house, and according unto thy word shall all my people be ruled: only in the throne will I be greater than thou"* (Gen. 41:40). Likewise Christ is sitting on the right hand of the Father (Rom. 8:34; Eph. 1:20; Col. 3:1).

28. Joseph was given great riches (Gen. 41:42-43). Jesus Christ is full of great riches. *"In whom we have redemption through his blood, the forgiveness of sins, **according to the riches of his grace**"* (Eph. 1:7, emphasis mine).

29. Joseph was hailed as a great ruler, many shouting out, "Bow the knee" (Gen. 41:43). The Bible says concerning Christ, *"That at the name of Jesus every knee should bow, of things in heaven, and things in earth, and things under the earth; And that every tongue should confess that Jesus Christ is Lord, to the glory of God the Father"* (Phil. 2:10-11).

30. Joseph was given a name that is above every name (Gen.41:45); likewise, concerning Christ, *"Wherefore God also hath highly exalted him, and given him a name which is above every name"* (Phil. 2:9).

31. Joseph was the Revealer of Secrets (which is what his new name meant in Hebrew); Christ was the Revealer of Secrets for all of mankind. *"For I have not spoken of myself; but the Father which sent me, he gave me a commandment, what I should say, and what I should speak"* (John 12:49). He was the Revealer of Secrets to the Apostle Paul. *"But I certify you, brethren,*

that the gospel which was preached of me is not after man. For I neither received it of man, neither was I taught it, but by the revelation of Jesus Christ" (Gal. 1:11-12). He is the Reveler of Secrets concerning the end of the world. *"The Revelation of Jesus Christ, which God gave unto him, to shew unto his servants things which must shortly come to pass"* (Rev. 1:1).

32. Joseph was given a Gentile wife (Gen. 41:45); the Bride of Christ, the church, is composed of both Jews and Gentiles. Thus Christ took unto Himself a Gentile Bride (see Eph. 5).

33. Joseph was thirty years old when he began his life as a ruler in Egypt (Gen. 41:46); Christ began His earthly ministry when he was thirty years old (Luke 3:23).

34. Joseph warned of the coming danger, urging his listeners to make preparations for the years ahead. Jesus Christ warned of the dangers of unbelief, hypocrisy, and pride, and spoke of the consequences of hell. He urged His listeners to make

preparations for the next life. Joseph could say, "If you do not prepare now, you will perish in the famine." Jesus said, *"Except ye repent, ye shall all likewise perish"* (Luke 13:3).

35. Joseph had power and provision. When people came to Pharaoh, desiring bread, he said to them, *"Go unto Joseph; what he saith to you, do"* (Gen. 41:55). What a perfect parallel of Christ's miracle-working power; His mother Mary told the servants at the wedding of Cana, *"Whatsoever he saith unto you, do it"* (John 2:5).

36. The seven years of famine are a perfect type of the seven years of tribulation; the famine was all throughout the land of Egypt (Gen. 41:56). Egypt is always a picture of the world; thus the entire world will be engulfed in the tribulation.

We will now look at Joseph's brethren, and how they typify the nation of Israel. The astounding parallels continue.

36. Joseph's brethren were driven out of their own land (Gen. 42:1-3). Arthur Pink points out the parallel here: "Just as a few years after his brethren had rejected Joseph, they were forced by a famine (sent from God) to leave their land and go down to Egypt, so a few years after the Jews had rejected Christ and delivered Him up to the Gentiles, God's judgment descended upon them, and the Romans drove them from their land, and dispersed them throughout the world."

37. Joseph was not recognized by his brethren (Gen. 42:6-8); likewise, when Christ came as the Jews' Messiah, they did not recognize Him as their Messiah, but rejected Him altogether (John 1:11).

38. Joseph punished his brethren. He falsely accused them, cast them into prison, and even bound one of them (Gen. 42:9-24). God had to punish the nation of Israel

for her unbelief and faithlessness to her Lord. Just as Joseph spoke roughly to his brethren, so God has dealt with Israel very roughly because of her sins.

39. Joseph tested his brethren, just as the Lord many times tested the nation of Israel. *"If ye be willing and obedient, ye shall eat the good of the land: But if ye refuse and rebel, ye shall be devoured with the sword: for the mouth of the LORD hath spoken it"* (Isa. 1:19-20).

40. Joseph would not let his brethren go until one of them was bound; this is the principle of substitution. Simeon was bound (Gen. 42:24) so the others could go free. Christ was our Substitute, bound to the cross, in order that we could go free (II Cor. 5:21; Gal. 3:13).

41. Joseph made provision for his brethren all along their journey. He provided corn for them and restored all their money in order that they would have provision "for the way" (Gen. 42:25). Thus the nation of Israel, while severely chastised by God,

has seen God's mercy and provision all along the way.

42. Joseph was made known unto his brethren the second time (Acts 7:13). When they first saw him, they had no clue who it was; but the second time they came to him, all was revealed. When Jesus came as the Messiah, the Jews rejected Him; but the second time He comes (The Second Coming) He will be received by His people and they will recognize Him as their Messiah and King.

43. Joseph graciously made a feast for his brethren and ate with them (Gen. 43:16); likewise Jesus was gracious to eat with publicans and sinners (Mark 2:16).

44. Joseph wept over his brethren several times, and specifically he wept over Benjamin (Gen. 43:30); Jesus Christ had the same compassion as He wept at the tomb of Lazarus (John 11:35) and over the city of Jerusalem (Matt. 23:37).

45. Joseph's brethren confessed their guilt before God (Gen. 44:16); in dealing with

Israel, God wanted her to recognize her guilt before a Holy God (see Ezek. 20:42-43; Hos. 5:15). Israel will be ready to turn to the Lord by the time Christ returns.

46. When Joseph revealed himself, his brethren were at first troubled, then comforted by his gracious kindness to them (Gen. 45:3-5); one day God will show great mercy and grace to the nation of Israel (see Isa. 54:7-8).

47. Joseph revealed his plan to his brethren: *"And God sent me before you to preserve you a posterity in the earth, and to **save your lives** by a great deliverance"* (Gen. 45:7, emphasis mine). The parallel is glorious! Jesus Christ was sent "before us" to the cross in order to save our lives by a great deliverance. *"Wherefore he is able also to save them to the uttermost that come unto God by him, seeing he ever liveth to make intercession for them"* (Heb. 7:25).

48. Joseph sent his brothers to tell their father the good news (Gen. 45:13); Jesus

has sent us with some Good News too. *"Go ye therefore, and teach all nations, baptizing them in the name of the Father, and of the Son, and of the Holy Ghost: Teaching them to observe all things whatsoever I have commanded you: and, lo, I am with you alway, even unto the end of the world. Amen"* (Matt. 28:19-20).

49. Joseph's brothers went forth proclaiming Joseph's glory (Gen. 45:13); they could say, "We have seen his glory." Concerning Christ, the Apostle John could say, *"And we beheld his glory..."* (John 1:14a). The Apostle Peter could say, *"Who by him do believe in God, that raised him up from the dead, and gave him glory..."* (I Pet. 1:21). The Apostle James called Him *"the Lord of glory"* (Jam. 2:1). Christ Himself prayed, *"And now, O Father, glorify thou me with thine own self with the glory which I had with thee before the world was"* (John 17:5). What a glorious Savior is our Lord Jesus Christ!

50. Jacob did not believe the news regarding

Joseph being alive (Gen. 45:26); when the women told the disciples that Jesus was alive, they likewise did not believe them (Luke 24:10-11).

51. Joseph had been dead in the mind of his father and his brethren for all those years; they considered him dead. Likewise the disciples knew that Christ was dead until He appeared before them.

52. Joseph made provision for his whole family in the land of Egypt (Gen. 46:6-7); likewise Christ has made provision for us through His own sacrifice. He has brought us out of the territory of sin and placed us "in Christ" (see Gal. 3:27; Rom. 8:1).

53. Joseph presented himself to his father (Gen. 46:29); Jesus Christ also presented Himself to the Father after His resurrection. Notice what He says to Mary: *"Touch me not; for I am not yet ascended to my Father: but go to my brethren, and say unto them, I ascend unto my Father, and your Father; and to*

my God, and your God" (John 20:17).

54. Joseph interceded on behalf of his family (Gen. 47:1); he was the mediator between his family and Pharaoh. Likewise Jesus Christ is our mediator: *"For there is one God, and one mediator between God and men, the man Christ Jesus"* (I Tim. 2:5). *"Who is he that condemneth? It is Christ that died, yea rather, that is risen again, who is even at the right hand of God, who also maketh intercession for us"* (Rom. 8:34).

55. Joseph gave bread to those who needed it, willing to negotiate and trade for it; he sustained the lives of countless souls (Gen. 47:15). Jesus Christ is the Bread of Life, ready to give life to anyone who will accept Him (John 6:35).

56. Joseph became the savior of the world as he provided for families with great concern and care for them; thousands of people flocked to him, and he was always willing to provide for them. *"Thou hast saved our lives,"* they cried (Gen. 47:25).

In an even greater way, Jesus Christ has become the Savior of the world. *"For God so loved the world, that he gave his only begotten Son, that whosoever believeth in him should not perish, but have everlasting life"* (John 3:16). The people of Samaria recognized Him as their Savior: *"for we have heard him ourselves, and know that this is indeed the Christ, the Saviour of the world"* (John 4:42b). *"Him hath God exalted with his right hand to be a Prince and a Saviour, for to give repentance to Israel, and forgiveness of sins"* (Acts 5:31). *"For therefore we both labour and suffer reproach, because we trust in the living God, who is the Saviour of all men, specially of those that believe"* (1 Tim. 4:10). *"And we have seen and do testify that the Father sent the Son to be the Saviour of the world"* (I John 4:14). This is the point in which Joseph is the best type of Christ; he pictured Christ not as a prophet, or a priest, or a king, but as a Savior, and even greater than that, the Savior of the world!

57. Joseph's brethren fell down and worshiped Joseph, exclaiming, *"Behold, we be thy servants"* (Gen. 50:18). Jesus Christ was also worshiped (Matt. 2:2, 8:2, 9:18, 14:33). Only God is worthy of worship, and Jesus even said so (Matt. 4:10). God clearly stated He would not share His glory or worship with anyone (Isa. 42:8), yet He shares both with Christ. So we can deduce that Christ is God.

58. Joseph was reconciled to his brothers; they repented of what they had done to him, and he graciously forgave them (Gen. 50:20). With salvation, the sinner is finally reconciled to Jesus Christ. *"And all things are of God, who hath reconciled us to himself by Jesus Christ..."* (II Cor. 5:18a). *"And you, that were sometime alienated and enemies in your mind by wicked works, yet now hath he reconciled..."* (Col. 1:21).

Thus we have seen the fullest and most perfect type of Christ in the entire Bible. The life of Joseph is remarkable, not for the fact that the story is gripping and touching, but for the fact that his life pictures the Savior of the world. Only an Almighty God could produce such a masterpiece as this!

Get the Whole Series!

Now Available!
Becoming a Man After God's Own Heart:
A Study on the Life of David

Coming Soon!
Becoming a Man of Leadership:
A Study on the Life of Moses

Becoming a Man of Courage:
A Study on the Life of Joshua

Becoming a Man of Wisdom:
A Study on the Life of Solomon

Becoming a Man of Prayer:
A Study on the Life of Daniel

Becoming a Man of Missions:
A Study on the Life of Paul

The *Becoming a Man* series by Paul E. Robinson is devoted to men of all ages. These books are a great resource to help encourage and equip Christian men with practical life teaching and powerful spiritual guidance straight from the lives of the Bible's greatest men.

Made in the USA
Las Vegas, NV
06 February 2022